YORKSHIRE

BURNLEY

LEEDS

LACKBURN

D0996801

JRD

HALIFAX

HUDDERSFIELD

LTON

OLDHAM

SADDLEWORTH

MANCHESTER

ASHTON UNDER LYNE

STALYBRIDGE

DUKINFIELD

STOCKPORT

SHEFFIELD

ALDERLEY EDGE

MACCLESFIELD

DERBYSHIRE

0   10
                          Miles

R. Derwent

THE
Summers
— OF —
Shotton

Best Wishes

THE
Summers
— OF —
Shotton

BRIAN REDHEAD
&
SHEILA GOODDIE

Sheila Gooddie

Brian Redhead.

Hodder & Stoughton
LONDON SYDNEY AUCKLAND TORONTO

British Library Cataloguing in Publication Data

Redhead, Brian
  The summers of Shotton.
  1. Summers, *(Firm)* 2. Businessmen—
  Great Britain—Biography 3. Steel
  industry and trade—Wales—Shotton
  (Clwyd)—History 4. Shotton (Clwyd)
  —Industries—History
  I. Title II. Gooddie, Sheila
  338.7′669142′0922   HD9521.9.S9

  ISBN 0 340 26911 1

CONTENTS

Illustrations

The illustrations in this book come from the archives of the British Steel Corporation Strip Products Group Records Centre at Shotton Works, with the exception of the following which are produced by permission of: members of the Summers family (pages 67, 76, 77, 82, 83, 91, 99, 100, 108, 110); Clwyd Record Office (pages 86, 88, 95, 106); Stalybridge Local Studies Library (pages 14, 15, 52).

Acknowledgments

The authors wish to thank: members of the fourth generation of the Summers family, in particular Peter Summers, without whose help this book could not have been written, and Anne Lake, who gave family photographs and reminiscences.

Employees of British Steel at Shotton, in particular Gordon Smith, his secretary Iris, and Terry Whitehead who searched out photographs and documents and were always very welcoming.

People who talked of their lives at Shotton – Ivor Jones, Eddie Mullen, George Millington, Arthur Joynson, Mr and Mrs Gamblin and Roy Phillips.

Stalybridge Local Studies Library.

Paul Mason, Archivist at Clwyd Record Office, Hawarden.

J. Gordon Read, Keeper of Archives, National Museums & Galleries of Merseyside.

Wilmslow Library.

Mr Francis Noel Lees, lecturer at Manchester University, who, before his death, found time to talk about George Gissing.

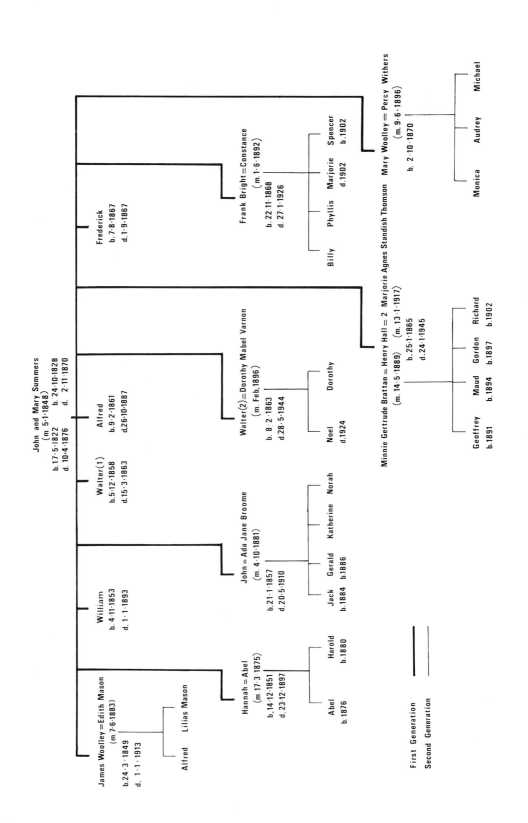

John and Mary Summers
(m 5·1·1848)
b.17·5·1822   b. 24·10·1828
d. 10·4·1876   d. 2·11·1870

James Woolley = Edith Mason
(m 7·6·1883)
b.24·3·1849
d. 1·1·1913

Alfred   Lilias Mason

William
b. 4·11·1853
d. 1·1·1893

Walter(1)
b.5·12·1858
d.15·3·1863

Alfred
b.9·2·1861
d.26·10·1887

Frederick
b. 7·8·1867
d. 1·9·1867

Frank Bright = Constance
(m. 1·6·1892)
b. 22·11·1868
d. 27·1·1926

Billy   Phyllis   Marjorie   Spencer
d.1902   b.1902

Hannah = Abel
(m 17·3 1875)
b.14·12·1851
d. 23·12·1897

John = Ada Jane Broome
(m. 4·10·1881)
b.21·1·1857
d.20·5·1910

Walter(2) = Dorothy Mabel Varnon
(m. Feb, 1896)
b. 8·2·1863
d.28·5·1944

Mary Woolley = Percy Withers
(m. 9·6·1896)
b. 2·10·1870

Abel
b.1876

Harold
b.1880

Jack
b.1884

Gerald
b.1886

Katherine

Norah

Noel
d.1924

Dorothy

Monica   Audrey   Michael

Minnie Gertrude Brattan = Henry Hall = 2   Marjorie Agnes Standish Thomson
(m. 14·5·1889)   (m. 13·1·1917)
b.25·1·1865
d.24·1·1945

Geoffrey   Maud   Gordon   Richard
b.1891   b.1894   b.1897   b.1902

First Generation ▬▬▬▬▬

Second Generation ─────

Foreword

This is the story of a family, not the story of a family business. The business, it is true, determined the lives of all the members of the family, those who were its casualties no less than those who adorned it. Some of them found it rewarding, some found it inhibiting, some could not wait to get away from it. It was the condition of all their lives, and this is the story of those lives.

It is the story as they left it, either in the public accounts of their known activities, or in the letters and diaries which they chose to leave behind. They did not write with an eye to posterity. It is to their credit that they were not so vain. They were not creators of an archful archive constructing a monument by which they would be remembered. They left their letters in the attic and it was there that they were found.

Nor, for better or worse, is this a contrived story, padded out with surmise or speculation or psychological guesswork. It is more in the nature of a family album, a collection of what happens to be remembered, and it is all the more truthful for that. It adds up to a remarkable chronicle, at one and the same time universal, typical, and unique.

It is a universal story in the sense that it is the story of every family, and everyone who reads it will recognise his or her family in it. The circumstances of course will be different, the happenings, the events, the accumulated wherewithal, but the responses aroused will be familiar, the responses to success, to failure, to achievement, to loss. In the Summers family, as in every family, there are the prudent ones and the feckless ones, the cautious ones and the reckless ones, the kind, the mean, the wise and the wanton.

It is a typical story in the sense that every successive generation is very much of its generation. The Victorian founding father has the simple certainty of his time with no desire other than to build a business and a family and to keep firm control of both. The ambitions of his seventh son, the Edwardian father figure, are more complex, and his second marriage to a chorus girl is a comic lapse. Here was a father who could give his children everything but confidence. So that third generation, though well-to-do, is ill-prepared for a business which it sees as an inheritance and a duty, but not as a calling. And yet they were better at the business than their self-doubt would suggest. And it is not stretching things to see in the story of the Summers family a portrait of the rising and falling fortunes of British industry. Certainly the trappings are a social history, the solid house and Sunday suit of the founder, the country homes of the Edwardians, the racing cars at Brooklands in the thirties.

But in the end this is a unique story because what happened to the Summers of Shotton, their triumphs and their sorrows, happened only to them. Their wealth and their social position, which they did not flaunt, could not protect them from anxiety and even less from accident. They had their share of tragedy as well as of happiness. And in their response to both it is impossible not to like them.

This is their story.

ONE

The Founding Father

John Summers left Bolton in 1842 to better himself. He was twenty and the son of a weaver. It had not been a good year for weaving, but then it seldom was. To be a weaver in Lancashire in the 1840s was to live in poverty and squalor and near-starvation, which was why John chose not to follow his father's trade.

His father was a widower. His name too was John, and he had married a girl called Hannah in 1813. Neither could read or write so they signed the register at Bolton Parish Church with a cross and then returned to worship at Bridge Street Wesleyan Chapel. It was there that their six children were baptised: Mary in 1815, Sarah in 1817, a first Elizabeth (who died in infancy) in 1819, a second Elizabeth in 1820. John, the only son, was born on 17 May 1822, and there was a sixth and last child who was born and buried on 2 February 1823.

Hannah, their mother, died soon after. An entry in the Burials Register of Bridge Street Wesleyan Chapel for 23 July 1823 reads: 'John Summers wife buried 6s., taking bier 3s.6d.' The grave numbers suggest that she shared her final resting place with the baby who had died five months earlier, for whom the burial fee was 3s. The graveyard no longer exists. It has long since been acquired by property developers, who safeguarded the inscriptions on the gravestones until a fire scarred beyond legibility the stones of the early 1820s.

The twenty-year-old John Summers who set off from Bolton in 1842 had therefore never known his mother, who had died when he was one. But that had not held him back. Not for him the weaving shed and the weeks off work. In his old age he claimed that he had been his own master from the age of fifteen. No record remains of how he had made his living in Bolton, but when he moved from there to Dukinfield, thirty miles away, he set himself up as a clogmaker.

He had crossed from industrial Lancashire into industrial Cheshire, to that north-west corner of the county which pushes into the Pennines. Dukinfield lay in a rapidly developing industrial valley in the shadow of Saddleworth Moors, where four counties met. Engels looked down on it in 1844 and described what he saw in his book, *The Condition of the Working Class*.

> A few streets lie in the narrow valley bottom, most of them run criss-cross, pell-mell, up hill and down, and in nearly all the houses, by reason of this sloping situation, the ground floor is half-buried in the earth; and what multitudes of courts, back lanes and remote nooks arise out of this confused way of building may be seen from the hills . . .

The people who inhabited this confusion wore clogs, the best protection against the muddy lanes and cold stone floors. Clogs were inexpensive yet strong, weather-proof and long-lasting. They could be handed down in the family when feet outgrew them, and they could be taken back to the clogger to be mended time and time again. It was no wonder that John Summers found that trade was brisk when he opened his first shop at the corner of Wharf Street and Crescent Road, next to the Lamb Inn.

The 1840s saw the opening of many small clogging businesses. Cloggers were regarded as skilled craftsmen for it took at least a year to learn to cut out the wooden soles correctly. Shaping the leather uppers was a more skilled craft and took much longer to perfect. Iron nails were hammered in to hold the two together and then covered with a narrow strip of leather that was stitched in place with waxed gut thread. On the wooden soles were nailed thin iron bars, curved to match the contour of the clog. Two crescent-shaped bars were needed for each clog and four made up a set. These irons, as they were called, kept the wooden soles from getting wet and from wearing down too quickly. They could be replaced as needed, and new irons and new nails were part of the clogger's daily trade, as were iron toe tips that gave extra protection to the clogs.

The Lamb Inn was next to John's first shop in Dukinfield.

John had many competitors such as James Smith who sold clogs in Market Street.

We do not know where John Summers learned his trade, but we do know that when he came to Dukinfield he was his own master. In his little shop, he sold his clogs on the ground floor, while the cellar was used for manufacture and repair. But life, even then, was not all work. At the end of a working day John would stroll not to the Lamb Inn next door, but to the Buck Inn in the High Street. The landlord's daughter had taken his fancy. Her name was Mary Woolley and John started courting her. They were married at Stockport Parish Church on 5 January 1848.

In the marriage register John's father gave his trade as clogger. We do not know whether he turned to clogging before or after his son, but no doubt he watched with pride as John's business expanded. The newly-wed couple set up house above the shop; John was twenty-five and Mary nineteen. She still helped out at the family pub, but she wanted to assist her husband and took on the job of keeping the accounts for him.

John bought the irons for his clogs from Giles Potter who had a clog iron business in the next street. Potter was no business man, given to spending his money before he had earned it. The time came when his debts grew too big for him to handle, and here was John's big chance. John bought him out and began to make clog irons and nails for himself, taking on extra hands to cope with the new work. Before long he was selling irons and nails to other clogmakers in the town and he engaged a travelling salesman, John Clark, to take new orders and settle payments.

John's business prospered. He could sell more nails than he could make at present, and the sale of clogs was a steady trade.

It was 1851, the year of the Great Exhibition in London. An enormous domed building of glass and iron was erected in Hyde Park and on 1 May, after a night of heavy rain, the Crystal Palace opened its doors to the crowds who were waiting in fitful sunshine to view the wonders of the age. The exhibition caught the imagination of the people who came from the farthest corners of the country and from overseas; altogether six million passed through the doors before they closed on 15 October. There was fear among some that the working classes who came on the cheap days – Mondays to Thursdays when admission was reduced to one shilling after the third week – would cause rowdiness and vandalism, but it was not so.

Mr Cook of Thomas Cook, who was an agent for the Midland Railway, organised excursion trains from many northern towns to the Great Exhibition, and it may be that John travelled to London on one of these. He stepped inside the Crystal Palace and made his way to the machinery section. As he walked around some of the nineteen thousand exhibits, he came across a nail-making machine which had earned its place in the exhibition, according to the catalogue, for its 'novelty, utility and economy'.

John needed no telling. The machine cost £40, which was every penny he had, but he did not hesitate. He bought it there and then and arranged for its carriage back home to Dukinfield.

There was one small problem: he had no money left to install the new machine. He confessed as much to his travelling salesman, John Clark. So Clark rushed round, bringing in new business and making old debtors settle so that they might lay the new engine bed.

Now the production of nails increased enormously and John Summers was delivering all over Lancashire and Yorkshire and into North Wales. He was well-placed, because the Sheffield, Ashton-under-Lyne and Manchester Railway had a branch line that passed through Dukinfield to Stalybridge, and the canal went from Ashton to Huddersfield.

It was time to look around for larger premises, and on 1 May 1852 John signed a lease with Mr Thomas Dearnaley for seven years, with the power to purchase at the end. Sandy Bank Iron Forge, only half a mile away, had the added advantage of a row of three houses, and it was into one of these that John moved with his family, which now included two children.

John concentrated on the production of irons and nails. Even with the new machine, nail-making was still hard work. The iron sheets were brought on

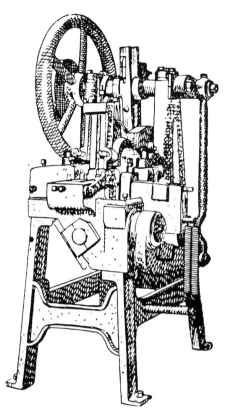

A nail–making machine similar to that bought by John at the Great Exhibition in 1851.

horse-drawn carts from the railway station, which was fortunately only a few hundred yards away from the works. Once in the nail shop the sheets were sheared into strips, six to twelve inches long, and a little wider than the length of a nail, so that there was enough iron for the nailhead. The iron was cut red hot, while it was soft and malleable, and boys and women sweltered in the heat alongside the men.

Geoffrey Hill, the poet, has described such a nail shop in which his grandmother spent her childhood: 'the nailshop stood back of the cottage, by the fold. It reeked stale mineral sweat. Sparks had furred its low roof. In dawnlight the troughed water floated a damson bloom of dust.'★

John's nail shop made money and by 1855 the profits came to one thousand pounds.

John's prosperity was part of the growing industry around him. In 1854 a new bridge was built over the River Tame between Dukinfield and its more

★ *Mercian Hymns* (André Deutsch, 1975).

In 1852 John moved to larger premises and a picture of the new works headed his business notepaper.

affluent neighbour, Ashton-under-Lyne, replacing stepping stones that had once forded the river. It was named the Alma Bridge, to commemorate the Battle of Alma fought on 20 September of that year, and it was officially opened in December 1855. It was free to foot passengers, but a toll was levied on carts and carriages. The street names of Dukinfield too, as of towns throughout the land, honoured the memory of thousands of British soldiers who had died in the Crimean War. John's forge backed down to Malakoff Street.

Sandy Bank Forge was given the grand title of Sandy Vale Cut & Patent Wrought Nail & Clog Iron Works. John conducted his business correspondence on smartly headed paper that carried a picture of the new works, all of which made a great impression on customers and colleagues in the iron trade. John Summers was obviously a man to watch.

As work expanded, John added to his workforce and by 1863 about twenty boys were making clog irons and nails for him. This was the year that nine-year-old Joe Fawley started to work for Summers. Joe's day began at six in the morning and ended at six in the evening. There was a half-hour break for breakfast and an hour for dinner. At the end of the week, he had earned 2s. 6d.

Men came as boys and stayed a lifetime at the Summers Works. Joe Fawley stayed until he was eighty. Men brought their brothers, their sons and even their daughters. It became a family tradition in Dukinfield to work for Summers and many lived just across the road in Summers Street, or round the corner in Summers Yard, or in one of the other narrow, grimy streets close by the works. In spite of its grand name, everyone knew it as Summers.

Albert Saxon started as a grinder on 2s. 6d. a week plus a bonus of 2s. 6d. for every ton of nails. He and his family could point with pride to a total of nearly four hundred years of service at Summers.

As John's workforce grew, he decided it was time to take on a manager for his nail shop. In 1864 Edward Shirley was hired for the job.

John Summers was a stern master but his employees knew where they were with him. The company rules drawn up in 1866 hung in the works for all to

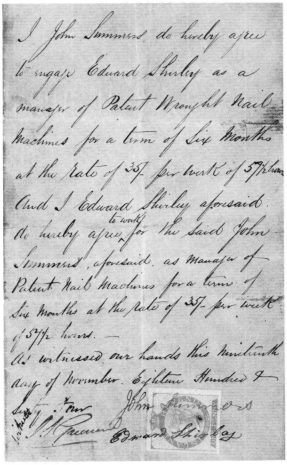

The agreement John made with Edward Shirley who in 1864 was engaged as manager of the nail shop.

see. Unpunctuality, extravagant use of oil and grease, horseplay, all were punished but none more rigorously than drunkenness at work. John Summers abhorred it.

It is said in the family that he had a half-brother called Ralph who was fond of his drink. John found him drunk in the works and told him never to darken the doorstep again. He never did and nothing more was heard of him.

John drew up rules for his workers with fines for misconduct.

John's immediate family prospered and grew. His wife, Mary, had a baby every other year. The first two were born in their rooms above the little shop in Wharf Street; the other nine in the house adjoining the Sandy Vale Works. Two of the eleven died in infancy, but the other nine were fine healthy children, and they spilled over into the second larger house, leaving a room for use as the office.

The third house was occupied by Jabez Pagden who was the works manager. So the family was surrounded by the works and their people. Indeed Mary was a great help to her husband in the early days, keeping the company accounts herself until child-rearing took up all her time.

The Summers family were certainly going up in the world. On Sundays, when Mary went out on John's arm, the neighbours took note. One such neighbour, Mrs Barlow, described the scene to her daughter.

> Mr and Mrs Summers went out together on Sundays. Mr S. in pot hat and tailcoat and Mrs S. in fine merino dress and the large bonnet of the day. In summer she wore a small silk shawl over her dress, fastened with a large handsome cameo brooch.

This was Sunday best wear. On a working day, John wore 'a vast blue lindsay apron, and large well polished clogs with brass tips'.

Mary herself was worn down with years of child-bearing. She confessed as much to a cousin in a letter which she wrote on 17 February 1868.

> Dear Cousin,
>   You will think me very dilatory in writing you but my late severe sickness left me weak for some time. I thank God that I can now go about the house comfortably but do not expect to go out much until after next month.
>   My son James (nearly 19) was so very anxious when I was suffering and still continues to be that he is desirous for me to be careful until April, perhaps not more so than the rest of the family but he is forward in expressing it. Mr Summers is well and active as usual . . . I have before me your kind letter of September 1st, the day on which our baby died. Perhaps the event was for the best as I have been enabled to take thorough rest in my weakness . . .

Mary needed all the rest that she could get in order to cope with her demanding family and her 'well and active' husband. Within days of writing that letter, she was to conceive again, and on 22 November 1868 another son was born, bringing the number of children to nine.

The family still lived in the house attached to the works, but John was thinking of moving his works to a new site. The introduction of rolling mills

Nine of John's eleven children were born in the house adjoining the Sandy Vale Works.

had convinced him that he must move to larger premises so that he could forge his own iron and roll his own iron bars. He realised that he could not continue with the old method of hammering iron by hand. There was, however, no more room at Sandy Vale. The workers were housed in Summers Street and Summers Yard, close to the works entrance, and there was no spare ground for expansion, so John planned to build an iron forge only a few hundred yards away, on Bayley Fields in Stalybridge. The buildings were of light iron structure standing on solid cast iron columns and the roofs were slated.

The local paper, the *Ashton Reporter*, was intrigued. On 2 January 1869, it wrote:

> On one or two occasions we have noted the progress of the Works in Bayley Fields or 'The Flats' as the locality is sometimes called. Mr J. Summers is erecting the only iron forge in the neighbourhood, upon a very extensive scale, and the works have been watched with much interest as the introduction of another branch of manufacture into the town.

It was watched with even greater interest when it all blew down. It was a Sunday afternoon and a freak gust of wind lifted the roof off the open shed and, according to the *Ashton Reporter*, 'carried it fourteen to fifteen feet'. John rushed to the scene with his seventh son Henry, who was then three years old. Young Harry remembered that afternoon all his life.

His father, he recalled, walked through the tangled ruins, picking up the pieces and confidently insisting that the work would be delayed for only two or three months, a prediction recorded in the *Stalybridge Reporter*. John was right: the shattered building was re-erected and the roof secured. The buildings for the nail works and the forge were ready at the same time.

In the new forge the cast iron was heated in a furnace, separate from the coke and coal. The molten metal was stirred continuously to allow the hot air to circulate through it; this was called 'puddling'. The carbon in the cast iron was oxidised and pure wrought iron remained; this was 'puddled iron' and the men who did this work were known as 'puddlers'.

Twelve puddling furnaces were erected and, many years later, Harry recalled the scene in his father's new works:

> . . . the furnaces were arranged in a semi-circle with the steam hammer in the centre of the diameter, radial plate ways leading to the furnaces. There were two trains of rolls driven by single cylinder condensing engines, the steam pressure was 60lbs, which was about the highest used in those days; the one engine drove the forge train where the blooms from the hammer were rolled out into puddled bars, the other engine drove the roughing and finishing rolls for the plate mill. The steam was supplied to the engines and

to the hammer by boilers attached to the furnaces, two puddling furnaces
to one boiler, one into each flue.

The opening of the Globe Iron Works was marked by due ceremony. The
workers formed a procession and were led round the town by a band, headed
by a large banner of sheet iron on which was a picture of a steam hammer and a
globe. John's workers, who included his men from the Sandy Vale Works,
were proud of their master and of their new works.

On the last day of 1869, a New Year's dinner was held at the Feathers Inn in
High Street, owned by one of John's relations. Fifty employees of the Globe
Iron Works were there. In the chair was Mr Griffiths, foreman puddler. He
proposed a toast in celebration of 'their new forge, good work and a
comfortable shop'. His toast was simple, 'Prosperity to the firm, and long
may Summers stand good'.

John himself was not present but he was represented by his eldest son,
James, who assured the assembled guests that his 'father's heart was entirely
with them'. The orchestra struck up the overture, 'The Caliph of Baghdad'.
Another toast was proposed, 'To the young master, and may he soon get
married'. To this the young master replied that nobody had asked him yet and
he did not think it would be soon – nor was it.

The men worked hard, twelve hour shifts were the practice, and John
prospered. His name had power and influence in the town. He had been an
active member on the town council for over ten years. His loyalties had always
been with the Liberals and he was known as a passionate admirer of Richard
Cobden and John Bright, giants of the Manchester political scene.

Alongside his growing industrial concern, he had found time to campaign
for the building of the smart new Mechanics Institute in the High Street,
which opened in 1862. Classes were held there every evening and were well
attended by the young men of Stalybridge and Dukinfield.

In 1868, as a Liberal Member of Dukinfield Council, John was voted on to
the committee that was formed to forward the idea of Public Baths, which
John keenly supported. In August he had gone with the mayor to see the Platt
family, tenants of Dunham Hall near Altrincham in Cheshire and wealthy mill
owners in their own right. The owner of Dunham, the seventh Earl of
Stamford and Warrington, owned considerable land around Ashton-under-
Lyne and Stalybridge. Many believed that it was due to John's eloquent
persuasion that Mr and Mrs Robert Platt offered to give the Baths to the town,
and their interest led to Mr Platt laying the foundation stone of the new Public
Baths on 24 October 1868. Eighteen months later came the opening
ceremony, and John was there. On 7 May 1870, he was appointed the first
chairman of the Baths Committee.

By this time Mary was again pregnant and on 2 October, 1870, their last child was born. Mary was exhausted from her years of child-bearing and she did not recover from the birth of her daughter. Exactly one month later, at the age of forty-two, she died. John, forty-eight, mourned her death and missed her loyal support. Mary had always been firmly behind his business ventures ever since the day that they set up home together above the cobbler's shop, next to the Lamb Inn, and in those early days, John had been grateful for Mary's neat handwriting and good book-keeping skills. She had borne him eleven children over nearly twenty-two years of marriage, and nine children lived on to be a great comfort to him. His ambitions had always been for his family, and now his responsibilities to his seven sons and two daughters spurred him on to greater efforts.

John's plans for expanding his works had always dovetailed neatly with his political activities, but now he was about to come into collision with the town council.

John had laid a tramway from his new works to the railway yard, so that the coal wagons could carry the coal straight into the works instead of his having to cart it from the railhead. The tramway crossed Russell Street, an unpaved road used by pedestrians.

On 6 January 1872, the council resolved to pave Russell Street, and gave Mr Summers notice to remove his tramway. Mr Summers refused. In a letter to the council he wrote, 'The freehold upon which the tramway is placed belongs

In 1869 John started to build the Globe Iron Works in Stalybridge and this was eventually the main entrance.

to Manchester, Sheffield & Lincs. Railway and the Corporation can't legally charge for its being there or insist on its removal.'

The local inhabitants took sides in the dispute. They wrote to the local paper: 'He has done a service to the town by laying the rails across the street,' said one. 'The working of Mr Summers' tramway is dangerous, and so much so that it is difficult to believe the owner has any regard for the limbs and lives of the passengers,' said another.

John felt that he had a perfect right to cross his own street with his traffic in a manner which he thought would cause least obstruction and nuisance to the public.

Tempers rose as the case dragged on for many months until the council's patience was exhausted and they resolved to take John Summers to law. This brought a howl of protest from eighteen hundred ratepayers, who signed a petition against the squandering of public money in unnecessary litigation.

The mayor was reported as saying:

> Mr Summers is determined to listen to nothing which opposes his rights over the surface of the street. It is well known that three or four wagons have gone off the rails and into the canal. This all arose from the tramway.

But when the suggestion was made that a committee should be set up to deal with Mr Summers' tramway, even the mayor thought enough was enough. 'The council,' he said, 'had tramway on the brain.' It had, and so it continued for eleven whole months.

Finally terms of settlement were drawn up and placed before the council at the November meeting. The mayor asked for the resolution to be accepted without discussion, at which point Councillor Marsland leapt to his feet and said:

> I do not care one single rushlight for the course Mr Summers has taken. I look on the question as one of principle. I am sorry that Stalybridge, a town so near to the cradle of free trade, should erect a monument of obstruction like that which we have under consideration.

Councillor Adshead, on the other hand, who was only too ready to obstruct John Summers, said:

> The whole of the costs ought to be paid by Mr Summers . . . Mr Summers has bragged that he would carry it to Parliament and I don't know where else, and that he would have a tramway in spite of all, and he had many thousands of pounds. I think we ought to pay not one single half-penny that he has driven us to incur.

One of John's supporters in the council said of the mayor: 'He seeks to cripple and destroy those who will not bow down and worship.'

When they had all stopped shouting, a vote was taken. The Conservatives and one Liberal (Councillor Heap) voted in favour of the terms of settlement. The rest of the Liberals voted against. The mayor declared the motion carried.

On 23 November the *Ashton Reporter* was able to report a settlement of the tramway litigation. John had his tramway but he had to pay £25 a year for the privilege. And for years after people talked about the Summers battle against the council.

In 1945, Mr Walter Kenyon, who worked for Summers, received a letter from his father-in-law, who wrote:

> I believe your firm had a struggle before they were allowed to make the level crossing in Bayley Street. As a lad I often watched 'Little Samson' pulling the waggons from the Works on to what was then the Manchester Sheffield & Lincs. Railway.

John celebrated the end of the struggle and his victory by moving house to the other end of the tramway from the Globe Iron Works. He bought Sunnyside, a large stone mansion of recent date, with stabling for three horses and carriages, and a large garden. He could walk through the garden, on to the railway line, into the goods yard and along the tramway to his works: not for him the country house. Sunnyside was opposite Whitelands Twill Mill.

But it was a fine house, and with Mary dead, John invited the children's nanny, Mrs Walker, a widow without children of her own, to move with them and take over the housekeeping and the cooking, with servants to help her.

She stayed with the Summers family all her life and retired when she was eighty to a small cottage in Stalybridge, sharing it with Sarah, another old and faithful servant.

And so by 1875, still only in his early fifties, the clogmaker of Dukinfield had become John Summers of Stalybridge, iron master and, it seemed, man of iron. He was the very picture of a successful Victorian industrialist – rich, respected and a realist. He lived where he worked, keeping a close eye on his works, his workers and his money.

But not for much longer. He was struck down that autumn by a brain haemorrhage. He lay for a little while, unlike himself, and died on 10 April 1876, five weeks short of his fifty-fourth birthday.

Stalybridge mourned his passing. They flew the flags at half-mast and waited to see what his children would make of the business.

There were nine of them, seven sons and two daughters. James, the eldest, was twenty-seven when his father died in 1876; the youngest, Mary, was five.

John moved his family from Sandy Vale to his new home, Sunnyside, which led directly to the railway and to the Globe Iron Works.

Two boys had died in infancy, Walter I in 1863 at the age of four and Frederick in 1867 at the age of barely four weeks.

James took on the role of family protector and provider. In due course he became the first chairman of John Summers & Sons and kept the chair until he died in 1913.

The seventh son, Henry, who was born in 1865, was destined to become the driving force in the family. But all of them were to have their share of success and sorrow.

TWO

The Children

James

James was the first-born and John's heir. It was always expected that he would go into his father's business as soon as he was old enough to help. No need for him to spend years on education as, later, brother William could. James' education was to be acquired in the iron and steel trade, and as long as his father was alive, James could be heir apparent without bearing too great a burden.

He was not a very sporty young man and the damp cold winters often brought coughs and colds that lingered on his chest. So much so one winter that the family doctor advised a long sea voyage as a cure and James was packed off on the sailing vessel *Sobraon* to Australia and back.

A family group. John is seated centre, his nine surviving children are (left to right) James, Alfred, Harry, William, Mary, Walter, Frank, John, Hannah. The identity of the elderly man is unknown but it could be John's father.

The journey took about ninety days in each direction so his father decided that it was time for brother John to come into the family business – not William, who was second in line. William's studies were considered far too important and he was gaining honours as a classical scholar.

John was brought from Owens College, where he had been quite over-shadowed by William's brilliance, and set to work learning about nail making. He proved so capable that the following year, when he was sixteen, Father had no hesitation in allowing James to go on another sea voyage.

The Globe Iron Works was booming and it was a smart move to send James to America to make contacts in the iron and steel trades and to see the latest machinery at work. On 29 March 1873, James, just twenty-four years old, set sail from Liverpool on the S. S. *Russia*, the same ship that had carried Charles Dickens home from America to Liverpool five years previously.

In the spring of 1868, Dickens had completed a reading trip through America and Canada, accompanied by George Dolby, his secretary and manager, and together they boarded the S. S. *Russia*, lying off Staten Island in New York Harbour, on 22 April. Friends and wellwishers accompanied them to bid them farewell and safe journey, among them Anthony Trollope, who had just arrived on the *Scotia* and hastened to the mail-tender to greet Dickens before he headed for home.

Dickens used his experiences of the voyage, among others, in his book, *The Uncommercial Traveller*, a collection of papers begun in his periodical *All the Year Round* in 1860 and continued over the years. In chapter thirty-one he wrote:

> Some halfyear ago, I found myself in my idlest, dreamiest and least accountable condition altogether, on board ship, in the harbour of the city of New York, in the United States of America. Of all the good ships afloat, mine was the good steamship *Russia*, CAPT.COOK, Cunard Line, bound for Liverpool. What more could I wish for?

James echoed these sentiments as he sailed leisurely down the River Mersey, bound first for Queenstown in Ireland where a few passengers were waiting to board the ship. He kept a diary of his journey.

The voyage itself was not without its humour and drama. Having nearly missed Queenstown through thick fog, the ship turned course westward and faced the force of the Atlantic waves. 'It was indeed a splendid sight. Ill as I was, I thoroughly appreciated it!' he wrote.

Once James had accustomed himself to the motion of the waves, he was able to join other hardy travellers in the dining saloon: 'It is very difficult to get your meals without some slight accident in the shape of a basin of soup being pitched into your lap or your iced water being upset on your pantaloons.'

Some days were calm, fine and warm and James could walk on deck, enjoying the sea breezes; other days he was forced to stay below as waves drenched the deck from stem to stern. After ten days at sea, he watched eagerly with the other passengers for the pilot who would guide them safely into harbour. He boarded the ship at 8.30 p.m., bringing news of the loss of the S. S. *Atlantic* off Halifax with 564 lives:

> He brought with him a newspaper containing a full account of the wreck, and details were read aloud in the saloon by one of the passengers. It caused us to be sincerely thankful for our safe arrival and we adopted a resolution to Captain Cook and his officers thanking them for their kindness and untiring exertions during our voyage. We let go our anchor about ten o'clock off Sandy Hook and remained there until morning.

Next day they arrived alongside the landing stage and went through 'the farce of having our luggage searched by the custom authorities . . . if the fellow won't take a dollar it's because he is seen and much regrets it.'

New York, the first American city that James saw, impressed him immensely: 'The main warehouses, hotels and public buildings, built of marble, are decidedly superior in appearance to anything to be seen in Manchester or elsewhere so far as my experience goes . . . You must remember in America they do things smart.'

From New York he travelled by the new Pullman train:

> It resembles more a drawing room than a railway car. Each carriage is divided into four compartments, the one at the end is the only one in which smoking is allowed. The seats are easy chairs which you can move to any position. Most agreeable. There are also elegant couches and mirrors from one end of the car to the other so that you may admire yourself during the entire journey. There is also iced water and wash stands, and it is altogether a most exquisite arrangement in the matter of railway travelling.

James took with him letters of introduction to people in the principal cities on his route. Many of them were business contacts in the iron and nail industries, but some were of social distinction. His short stay at Washington included a call at the White House:

> . . . but the President, not knowing of our coming, left last night for St. Louis. His secretary very kindly took us through the house and we were much pleased with the modesty and neatness of the furniture and decorations. We saw the bed which the Prince of Wales presented to the President when he visited Washington in 1859, and also a carpet sent by the

Sultan of Turkey. We also went through the Treasury, a very large and handsome building.

James expressed his 'liberal' views on emancipation:

> Washington contains a University for the education of coloured men and I am glad to find that the principal states are providing for the thorough education of the emancipated negroes . . . now let us hope in the course of a very short time they will be brought up in the full knowledge of what is required of them.

Not all of his impressions were favourable:

> Pittsburgh too much resembles our Sheffield and other steelmaking towns. But for the iron business operations I guess it is the finest in the States and doubtless will become in course of time a most important iron centre. The bituminous coal is used here exclusively which in a great measure accounts for its dirty appearance. I complained to a gentleman here of the quantity of smoke and he replied it was healthy. The hygienic properties of the Pittsburgh smoke was beneficial to health. He was connected with the iron trade.

Some people, as well as towns, he was glad to escape:

> Mr Heron of the firm of Dewry, Vance & Co. is very well posted in everything connected with the iron trade, and it is really wonderful the amount of knowledge some of these Americans carry about with them . . . He is supplied with maps, sections, descriptions and everything pertaining to iron and coal in the States and I had as much of all these as he could get into me during my two hours stay.

James sampled the river boats, sailing down the Ohio River on the steamer *Andes*, 'fare six dollars including meals and attendance':

> There is one objection to these river steamers and that is they often blow up. . . . On the first morning our captain was two sheets in the wind before breakfast and we were carrying 140lbs. pressure of steam in boilers made of plates ¼″ full. His certificate names the maximum pressure not to exceed 125lbs.

Notwithstanding James reached Louisville safely, and on to the Pullman again for St Louis, his destination being Iron Mountain where the quality of iron is 'the finest in the world containing 68% of iron.'

Friday morning, 9 May 1873, exactly a month after landing in America, James took the train for Chicago:

> It is almost impossible to realise the vast extent of the fire which ravaged the city in October 1871, yet with marvellous rapidity, the city has become even more prosperous and beautiful than ever. The cause of the vastness of the fire to a great extent was the great number of buildings erected of wood, but now the authorities will not permit any building of this material to be erected.

Some of his letters of introduction led to very pleasant encounters. After crossing Lake Michigan from Milwaukee, he reached Grand Rapids to make the acquaintance of Mr Lowe, who welcomed him to his home:

> They have a croquet lawn. Mr Lowe and I played many games and I enjoyed it. Miss Lowe often played with us and also the two Miss Graves . . . I do not feel cool enough to speak at present of their charms. Perhaps by the time I return I may be in a proper condition to write of them. I have a photo of one from which, however, you can form a very inadequate idea of her beauty.

His new friends had emigrated from Stalybridge: Mr Lowe's father-in-law had been one of the earliest pioneers about thirty years earlier, when the population consisted chiefly of Indians:

> I guess he is now very well-to-do. He intends in three weeks to sail for England in the *Cuba* with some of his family and I have invited them to call upon you, and should they do so before I return, I hope sister will kindly entertain them.

James thought it wise to warn his family that Mr Lowe's father-in-law 'is so deaf that you have to speak to him through a trumpet'.

During his stay at Grand Rapids, he was taken by Mr Lowe to inspect one of the city schools, which impressed him very much:

> I have come to the conclusion that the children of this Country have the means of education of a high character and they cannot but be benefited by it. Boys and girls, rich and poor are all together – there is no distinction – one is as good as another and no school fees.

By now it was mid-May and too hot to be pleasant. James was glad that he was not going south:

> . . . it becômes almost unbearable, particularly for those who are accus-
> tomed to a colder climate. It is told of one man during the war [American
> Civil War] who was visibly seen to be melting away when it was decided at
> once to pack up what was left of him in ice and send him home to
> Vermont.

James went on to Cleveland where he boarded the train for Oil City, then
Buffalo and on 24 May he reached the American side of Niagara Falls:

> . . . the more I gazed at them and the longer I stayed, so did I become more
> and more impressed with their magnificence and the grandeur of the
> spectacle . . . I felt extremely reluctant to leave the place.

James, however, had to keep to his schedule with appointments in Toronto.
Then followed one of the most exciting experiences of the whole trip,
shooting the rapids from Montreal:

> A fortnight previous a steam, owing to an accident to her engines, got
> stranded on a rock in passing through the Lachine Rapids . . . They had
> tried to blow her up but had not succeeded very well. She had on board at
> the time of the accident one hundred and fifty passengers who were all got
> off safely by the Indians in canoes . . . It is a trifle alarming to those not
> knowing the course of the current. You appear to be going direct for an
> island right in the middle of the river when all at once she turns swiftly
> round and you are told she passed between two rocks which do not give
> her more than a few feet on each side.

At last, with a sheaf of business contacts, some useful information on the iron
and steel business in America and a list of Americanisms to amuse the family,
'I guess I'll slide off . . .'
  'Aint it . . .'
  'Is that so . . .'
  'A right bright boy . . .'
James, a right bright boy himself, sailed for home.
  The death of his father in 1876 meant the acceptance of family duties and
responsibilities for James. Only he and brother John were in the works;
William was at London University, and the four younger boys were away at
school and college. James was diligent in seeing that they received the very
best education, as his father would have wished.
  James and John got on with the job of keeping the Globe Iron Works in
business. John married in 1881 and two years later James, now thirty-four,
married Edith, daughter of Hugh Mason, a successful businessman and

Member of Parliament for Ashton. It was a happy day for the people of Stalybridge.

Crowds gathered from early morning on 7 June to catch a glimpse of the honoured guests, and by the time of the wedding at quarter past eleven, the Albion Chapel was overflowing. People peered through the chapel windows to catch a glimpse of the seven bridesmaids dressed in pale coral pink and cream lace. One of the excited bridesmaids was James' young sister Mary, now twelve.

The bride wore ivory satin, on her arm a diamond and pearl bracelet, the gift of the groom, and round her neck a diamond pendant, the gift of her father.

A marquee had been set up in the grounds of the bride's home at Groby Hall and here the guests enjoyed a sumptuous wedding feast. The merrymaking lasted through the evening, with music provided by Mr Charles Hallé's band.

The workers of the Globe Iron Works were given a day's outing to Blackpool to celebrate their master's wedding. James and Edith set up home in Stalybridge and spent the next fifteen years there, until family developments brought about their removal to an imposing residence near Chester.

Hannah

Hannah was the second child of John Summers and was given the name of his mother. For eighteen years she was the only girl in a family of ever more boys, but when she was almost nineteen her mother gave birth to a second daughter, Mary. A month later on 2 November 1870 her mother died, whereupon Hannah took over the role of mother, with Nanny Walker to help her.

She was well prepared. In that letter to a cousin in 1868, her mother had said, 'Hannah enjoys good health, is very useful and good company for me.'

And it was she whom James had referred to when he wrote to his father from America, hoping that his sister would entertain the Lowes. He had no need even to ask, because Hannah was a great organiser all her life.

Hannah was the first of the family to marry. (James, the young master, was still waiting to be asked.) She was twenty-three and she married a man of forty, who in 1875, the year of their wedding, was the Mayor of Ashton.

His name was Abel Buckley and he and his older brother, Nathaniel, were bachelors and very wealthy. They owned Ryecroft Mill and Oxford Road Mill and Pennington Mills. Abel also owned most of Mayfield Printing Company and had interests in collieries in Denbighshire. He was a director of the Palace Hotel, Buxton, and a director of the Manchester and Liverpool District Bank.

He must have been quite a catch and certainly able to meet any obligations expected of him by Hannah's father. Yet the wedding on 17 March 1875 was strangely quiet. The locals had expected it to be at the chapel, where the family worshipped in Melbourne Street, Stalybridge, but the couple chose Albion Chapel, the Congregational chapel in Ashton-under-Lyne where Abel and many of his rich relations worshipped. Abel's brother Nathaniel had laid the foundation stone here as long ago as 1833, an act that was to be repeated by Abel when the new Albion Chapel was built in 1890.

Perhaps the confusion over the chapels explained the half-empty pews at the wedding, but this could not explain the absence of invited guests. And yet the ministers of both the chapels took part in the ceremony as though it were a much grander affair.

The time of the wedding was unusually early at 10 a.m. and by 10.30 a.m. the service was over. None of Hannah's family were present, apart from her father who gave the bride away. She was unattended, with no bridesmaids, and the groom had only his brother as best man with no groomsmen. The handful of guests, relations on Abel's side, returned to Hannah's home at Sunnyside for the wedding breakfast and afterwards Hannah, wearing a no-nonsense outfit of plain brown silk with a plainly trimmed bonnet, left with her new husband on the 12.40 London train for a honeymoon on the Continent.

This much was reported in the local paper, and the quietness of the wedding was noted, but no speculations were made, and nothing has since come to light to explain why Hannah's brothers stayed away from her wedding. But we do know that the honeymoon had to be prolonged in Italy, for Hannah was taken ill with what was officially described as 'Roman fever'. The newlyweds had planned to be on honeymoon for two months, but they were forced to be away from home an extra month.

It was a rule in Ashton Council that if the mayor were absent for longer than two months, this was sufficient grounds to declare the office vacant. When Abel was elected mayor in November 1873, the voting had been Conservative 15, Liberal 15. The casting vote by the Liberal mayor had made Abel his successor. Now the Conservatives took advantage of Abel's enforced absence abroad to oust him from office.

Although his new bride was seriously ill in Italy and unfit to travel, this was not regarded by his political enemies as reason to delay. The *Ashton Reporter* said of their action, 'It deserved to meet with universal and unmitigated reprobation.' Nevertheless at the special meeting called on 23 June 1875, by sixteen votes to eleven, Abel was voted out of office.

For Abel, and indeed for Hannah who swiftly recovered, it was no more than a temporary affront. They returned home to Moss Lodge, Ashton, and took up a life of social and political responsibility, a life of public work. Hannah found herself supporting worthy causes such as the Sick Nursing Association, which was newly formed and of which she became treasurer and, in due course, president.

She was often called upon to open bazaars, and in this way she became the first woman public speaker in the district. Her first political speech seems to have been unpremeditated. She was sitting by her husband, who had been accepted as Liberal candidate for the Prestwich division. Hannah spoke up in answer to a lady who had been supporting female suffrage from the floor of the meeting. Her actual words are unrecorded but, no doubt, she spoke in favour of women's emancipation.

Hannah was a willing and active worker in Abel's campaign to enter Parliament. When she married, she entered into a political family as strongly Liberal as her own had been. From the very first moment that Stalybridge and Dukinfield were allowed to send their own member to Parliament in 1868, Abel's brother, Nathaniel, had been the Liberal candidate and he was the elected Member from 1871 to 1874 when the Conservatives regained the seat.

Hannah enjoyed the cut and thrust of politics and made quite a name for herself, speaking from the Liberal platform. In 1880 brother William became Liberal MP for Stalybridge and Dukinfield and Hugh Mason, a relation by marriage, became Liberal MP for Ashton. Husband Abel had to wait until the next general election in 1885 to become Liberal MP for Prestwich.

Hannah's political fervour and behaviour persuaded other women to become involved and led to the formation of the Liberal Women's Association in Ashton, of which she became the first treasurer.

Her political stamina seems to have been greater than her husband's. He quickly became bored at Westminster by the endless debates on Home Rule for Ireland. In any case the Liberal government soon crumbled. They had been living dangerously, with no overall majority, and in 1886 they were defeated on their Irish Home Rule Bill. Abel lost at the next election and bowed out of politics.

For some time Abel had been a very wealthy man. In 1877 he and his brother Nathaniel had inherited Irish estates, which included Galtee Castle in the county of Cork, near Mitchelstown in south west Ireland. Nathaniel bought neighbouring land to add to their estates, while Abel invested in land near home on Saddleworth Moors. In 1879 he paid £13,730 for 1,454 acres with shooting rights, called Ashway Gap.

The rest of this inheritance passed to him in 1885 when his aunt died. Ryecroft Hall became his and he and Hannah moved from Moss Lodge to their new home. They lived there in great style with their two sons, Abel born in 1876 and Harold born in 1880. Brother William made it his home, too, when he was not at Westminster or abroad.

They entertained on a grand scale. In August 1887 they held a picnic for six hundred people at Ashway Gap, their Saddleworth estate. A marquee was erected and those who were invited said that the hospitality was 'sumptuous'. We do not know what the occasion was, whether private or public, local or even national celebration in honour of Queen Victoria's Golden Jubilee, but we do know that it was part of the pattern of their elegant and lavish lifestyle. More riches came their way when, on Nathaniel's death in 1892, Abel received his brother's share of their joint business ventures, plus £25,000.

They also gave generously. Especially favoured was the new Albion Chapel where Abel laid the foundation stone in September 1890. The building committee had good cause to be grateful to Abel and publicly expressed their thanks:

> It would have been impossible for the church and congregation to face this large expenditure but for the magnificent liberality of Mr Abel Buckley in making a gift of the tower and spire, at an outlay of £4,000, besides his large contribution to the general building fund.

When the chapel was completed in 1895, Abel provided the organ at a cost of 2,000 guineas.

Hannah was a good friend of the local hospital. In 1893 she gave her support to a cot in the children's ward at £30 a year and endowed one at £1,000 a year. She took a serious interest in the work of the Ashton Board of Guardians, which had been formed in 1834 to administer the Poor Law. The guardians maintained a workhouse for the poor of the parish and Children's Homes for the Poor Law children. Every Christmas, Hannah gave all one hundred and thirty children of the homes a new sixpence each.

Hannah still found time for her good works. She founded the Ashton branch of the NSPCC in 1893 and became its treasurer.

She also maintained her political interests, being vice-president of the Women's Liberal Federation and president of both Huddersfield and

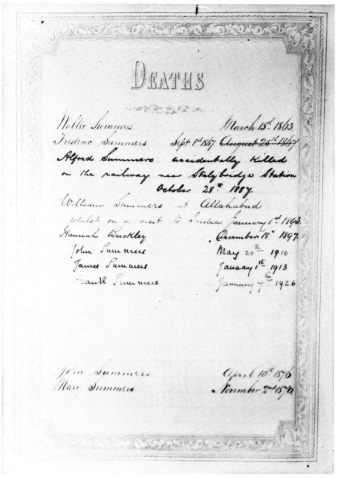

A page from the family Bible.

Droylsden Women's Liberal Associations. Perhaps she drove herself too hard, because when only forty-four she suffered a paralytic stroke.

But she made a good recovery and was able to keep up her visits to their Irish home. Christmas was often spent at Galtee Castle and it was there in December 1897 that Hannah caught a chill while out driving. There seemed to be no cause for alarm; indeed, Hannah was talking of going to the south of France for the worst of the winter, leaving after the New Year. However, bronchitis developed, Hannah suddenly took a turn for the worse, and with her husband and her two sons by her side, she died in the early hours of 18 December, aged forty-six.

William

William, born on 4 November 1853 and the second son of John Summers, was the scholar of the family. Like all the brothers who came after him, he was sent, at the age of ten, to boarding school, to Mr James Wood's school in Alderley Edge, Cheshire. James Wood was a Quaker and a Liberal who believed in the healthy mind in the healthy body. The advertisement for his school in *Morris' Directory* of 1874 read:

> . . . Ample provision is made to promote the healthy physical development of the boys. There are for the use of Pupils, a cricket ground, covered playground, bathrooms, carpenter's workshop and chemical laboratory.

English grammar, mathematics, natural history and outdoor games featured prominently on the timetable.

The domestic side of the school was looked after by the headmaster's wife and the boys' health was cared for by his sister, who was the official school matron. There was also an experienced nurse who had been with the Wood family, looking after their own seven children, for over twelve years. Parents could rest assured that their sons were in capable hands.

Twice a week the boys were allowed beyond the school boundaries and groups would set off on long walks to explore the disused copper mines on Alderley Edge, or to the pretty villages of Gawsworth and Chelford and the town of Knutsford. The caretaker's wife was allowed to sell sweets, cakes and drinks, which kept the boys within bounds for the rest of the week.

William stayed at Lindow Grove School for five years and became a star pupil. His parents must have been well pleased by his progress and were, no doubt, among those who could, 'bear willing testimony to the satisfactory results of the training of the boys whether tested by their sound scholarship or by their general development and refinement of character', as proclaimed in the school prospectus.

As soon as he was old enough, in 1867, brother John joined the school, and four years later it was the turn of Alfred.

Meanwhile, in 1868, just before his fifteenth birthday, William moved on to Owens College which was then in Quay Street, Manchester, in what had been the home of Richard Cobden.

The college was increasing in numbers with every passing year as more and more boys were prepared for the examinations of University College, London. The numbers had stood at 127 three years earlier and this had risen from 57 in 1860. And there were evening classes, too. In 1865 more students were being taught in Quay Street than were studying in the main departments of University College, London.

William seemed to collect prizes effortlessly during his years at Owens College. The list reads:

> Shuttleworth Prize (political economics)   £50 per annum for two years.
> Shakespeare Scholarship   £40 a year for two years.
> Wellington Prize (Greek testament)   £20.
> Shuttleworth History Prize.
> English Essay Prize.
> Early English Text Society's Prize.

It was not surprising that in the 1871 degree examination of University College, London, William gained an exhibition in English for £30 per annum for two years, and the next year took honours in logic and moral philosophy. At the same time he took his first LLB exam and took honours in jurisprudence and Roman law.

Then it was on to Oxford in 1874 and after three years he gained a BA with honours. The next year, 1878, saw him back at London University where he received a gold medal for his MA in classics and came fifth in the examinations for logic, philosophy and political economy.

Not bad going for the son of a clogger, whose illiterate grandparents had signed their wedding certificate with a cross. John Summers was justly proud of his student son and thought it was no trouble at all to fix up one of the rooms at home as a study, where William's privacy had to be respected by his seven younger siblings.

During his student days William never lost touch with his old school, and on visits there he was much admired by a contemporary of his younger brothers, John and Alfred. The admirer was a boy called George Gissing who, years later in an essay which he wrote called 'The Old School', said of William: 'We often saw him and I, for one, always gladly – he brought with him such a suggestion of hard study and brilliant success.'

George Gissing was the same age as William's brother John, while the two younger Gissing brothers, William and Algernon, were more of Alfred's age. They all attended Lindow Grove School at Alderley Edge, together with nearly sixty other boys. Reminiscing in his fictionalised autobiography, *The Private Papers of Henry Ryecroft*, George Gissing recalled: 'I can see the long school room, lighted by the early sun, I can smell the school room odour – a blend of books and slates and wallmaps and I know not what.'

But it was with William, four years his senior, that Gissing became friends. He followed William's path to Owens College in 1872, when he was fourteen and a half years old, and the next summer he visited William at the Summers' home Sunnyside in Stalybridge.

Gissing was a brilliant student and in his exams came first in the whole of England, which entitled him to three years' free tuition. His subjects were Latin, French and Greek so he and William shared their enthusiasm for the classics.★ They kept in touch while William was at Oxford and when their old headmaster moved house to Colwyn Bay, they went on a walking holiday together in North Wales and visited his home, Ty'n y Maes.

But Gissing's academic brilliance ended disastrously. He became friendly with a prostitute, Marianne Helen Harrison (Nell) and thought that by providing her with money he could change her lifestyle. He bought her a sewing machine as a way out of prostitution. But in helping her he got into financial difficulties and stole from fellow students. Books and coats disappeared from the cloakroom and a detective was set to watch for the thief and caught Gissing in the act.

Gissing was expelled from Owens College and served a short prison sentence, one month with hard labour. His friends stood by him and on his release from prison he was given the fare to America to make a fresh start. But within a year, in October 1877, he was back in England, living in mean apartments in London with his sweetheart Nell, whom he eventually married in October 1879.

While Gissing's career had foundered, William's had steadily risen. His father lived long enough to see his son at Oxford but died before William became either a Member of Parliament or a barrister.

1880 was a busy year for William. He was just beginning to make his mark in politics but he found time to call on Gissing on the publication of his first book, *Workers in the Dawn*, first to be published that is, although the second to be written (the first has completely disappeared). Gissing spoke of William with affection when he wrote to his brother Algernon in August of that year.

William was invited back to his old college in October 1880. He was the sort of student who brings honour and glory to seats of learning and he was asked to become a member of the newly created University Court. On 25 May 1880, Owens College had become, by Royal Charter, Victoria University.

Brothers Walter, seventeen, and Harry, fifteen, were now students at the Oxford Road building to which the college had moved from its cramped quarters in Quay Street in 1873.

★ Like his friend before him, Gissing was showered with academic prizes and, as John Stewart Collis tells us in his introduction to the 1982 edition of *The Private Papers of Henry Ryecroft* (Harvester Press), 'he received so many prizes on one occasion that he was obliged to hire a cab to take them back to his lodgings'.

But the political life beckoned William, and it seemed like a natural progression for one whose father had once walked all the way from Stalybridge to Rochdale to hear John Bright speak. William's home town of Stalybridge had only been created a borough with the right to send a Member to Parliament since 1868, when William was a boy of fifteen. The townspeople felt that they had waited long enough to become independent from their neighbours in Ashton-under-Lyne, who had been given a Member of Parliament as long ago as 1832.

In the 1868 election Nathaniel Buckley, later to become related through Hannah's marriage, stood as Liberal candidate against James Sidebottom who was to be the first Conservative MP for Stalybridge and Dukinfield, with a majority of 327. Four years later it was Nathaniel's turn to take the seat for the Liberals.

In those days elections were carried out in public on a platform known as the hustings. A number of flat-topped lorries were placed together on the Market Ground, the mayor presided and speeches were made. The result was on a show of hands. But that changed in 1872, when voting by ballot was introduced.

At the next election in 1874, Nathaniel Buckley lost to the Tories and the new MP was Mr T. H. Sidebottom (not related to the last Conservative MP). The new man was a wealthy cotton-spinning merchant. He became a good representative for Stalybridge and Dukinfield, his praises sung by all the locals, but his political views were the wrong colour for the Summers family.

William made his first political speech in 1876, while he was still a student at Oxford, and in 1878, while he was studying for his MA at London, he accepted the Liberal candidacy for Stalybridge. The general election was called in 1880 and the Liberals turned the Conservative majority in the Commons of forty-seven into a Liberal majority of fifty-one.

William was swept into office on the Liberal tide by 164 votes. The victory was described by one admirer as 'the triumph of David over Goliath', and indeed William was a young untried politician who had managed, after a hard fight, to unseat the established Conservative cotton industrialist.

He was a lively MP and became a good performer in the House. He must have inherited his father's restless energy because, the following year, he found time to read for the Bar and was called at Lincoln's Inn. He did not, however, go on to practise as a barrister, but returned to his career as a rising star in politics.

William spoke on many matters in the House, from powder magazines in the Mersey to the frontiers of Turkey and Greece. He made it his business to become knowledgeable in foreign matters. The *Manchester Guardian* said of him much later, 'his fluency never degenerated into either feebleness or flippancy'.

A FEW
HARD NUTS
For the Tories to Crack!

Who has repeatedly insulted Catholics and Nonconformists by his votes and his speeches?   T. H. SIDEBOTTOM.

Who puts on the screw and prevents parents sending their children to the School of their choice ?

T. H. SIDEBOTTOM.

Who charged his Weavers for Shuttles, Hand-brushes, &c. ?

T. H. SIDEBOTTOM.

Who was guilty of enforcing this practice which Judge Ellison described as unfair and illegal ?   T. H. SIDEBOTTOM.

Whose Factory always looks as if it were loosing ?

T. H. SIDEBOTTOM'S.

Whose Workpeople were so destitute that the Shopkeepers of Hadfield took compassion on them and sold them a 2lb. Loaf for a 1d. and Bacon at 3d. per lb. ?

T. H. SIDEBOTTOM'S.

Where can you find a Four-loom Weaver whose Wages have averaged only 11s. per week for the last two months ?

At T. H. SIDEBOTTOM'S.

Whose Workpeople were compelled to go round in the evenings to beg Bread for themselves and children ?

T. H. SIDEBOTTOM'S.

Working-men of Stalybridge and Dukinfield! Do not vote for the man who would grind down our wages until we are almost starving, but

VOTE FOR SUMMERS
The Friend of the Working Man !

Robert Phipps, Printer and Publisher, Astley-st., Dukinfield.

A contemporary political poster.

His speech on the second reading of Mr Gladstone's Irish Land Bill was received with such favour that he was invited to second the Address in answer to the Queen's Speech at the opening of the 1884 Session. A brilliant future was predicted for him.

But in the general election of 1885, he lost his seat by 219 votes to his old political rival, Mr T. H. Sidebottom. His opponent plastered Stalybridge and Dukinfield with posters. 'Vote for Sidebottom' they read, and vote for Sidebottom they did. 'The Friend of the Working Man' was ousted, beaten, it was claimed, because of boundary changes. William was not the only Liberal to fall; the pendulum had swung nationally in the Conservatives' favour, although they had no overall majority.

His family and friends and the workers of the Globe Nail and Iron Works were sorry to see William lose his seat, but they took the opportunity of celebrating the reputation of their local boy, who had become a great man. They held a tea party in his honour in the Mechanics Institute on 12 December 1885.

Four hundred workmen and their wives attended. Joe Fawley, who had been at the Summers works since he was nine and was now a member of the Globe Works Committee, presented William with an illuminated address. And the family was there in force – James, Hannah, John, Alfred, Walter and Harry. Only the two youngest, Frank and Mary, were absent.

While away from Parliament William put his time to good use. He travelled, often with his brother Alfred. They went as far as Egypt, Turkey and Greece and when they returned it was time for another election. It was 1886 and the government had been defeated on the Irish Home Rule Bill.

William was asked to contest various parliamentary seats and he eventually chose Huddersfield. He won by 184 votes, going against the national trend which returned the Conservatives with a majority of 116 – and they stayed in power for the next six years. In the general election of 1892 William was re-elected with an increased majority of 261.

By this time his reputation was confirmed and it was confidently predicted that he would shortly be offered a post in government. But he had not been too well during the election campaign and on several occasions his sister Hannah, only too pleased to be asked, had taken his place at public meetings.

Immediately after the election William went for a rest to Hannah's Irish home at Galtee Castle, and then he took the opportunity to visit India. He thought the trip might do him good and it provided a chance to brief himself thoroughly on the Indian question, which would give him an advantage over many in the House on his return, when foreign affairs were debated.

He sailed for Bombay on 27 October 1892, having paired with the Conservative MP for Prestwich until 8 February. During his Indian tour he delivered an address on the British Empire to two hundred students at the American Mission School at Lahore. His main purpose, however, was to attend as a visitor the annual meeting of the Indian National Congress to which he had been invited. He hoped to make the acquaintance of some of the leading members of the Indian community, and he took with him letters of introduction from England.

On New Year's Eve Hannah received a telegram from India that read, 'Mr Summers dangerously ill: malignant smallpox. Civil Surgeon.'

William had not been vaccinated – in fact he had been a supporter of the anti-vaccination lobby, who agreed with parents' rights to withhold vaccination from their children.

Local authorities had been dealing with various aspects of health and sanitation for over twenty years; indeed, as early as 1848 local Boards of Health had been formed, following an outbreak of cholera in the country. These were voluntary establishments under the central Board of Health and opposition from critics of centralisation led to the Board being dispersed to various government departments. Another wave of cholera in 1865–66 compelled the government to provide sewers and a good water supply, and local authorities to appoint sanitary inspectors.

State vaccination had been a continuous activity since well before William became an MP; it was compulsory but parents could register as 'conscientious objectors' and the rich could avoid it by paying a fine. This was resented by the working man and William took his side.

Now he had smallpox and, within twenty-four hours of Hannah receiving the news, he was dead. It was New Year's Day, 1893, and William was buried at Allahabad. He was thirty-nine.

People at home were shattered by the news, and tributes poured in from all levels of society in which William had mixed so easily for such a short time. His political opponent from past contests in Stalybridge spoke the thoughts of many:

> I have had the misfortune to differ from him in politics but cannot refrain from saying that I most deeply and sincerely lament and deplore his loss. He was always a most powerful and formidable opponent, but after the battle, was ever ready to shake hands and be friends. He had the possibilities of a great and, perhaps, a very great future before him.

In April of that year, 1893, sister Hannah wanted to collect his literary and political papers and publish them. She contacted Gissing, and they met at Torquay to discuss an introduction to be written by Gissing, who had told her that he was delighted to participate and wanted no fee. Alas, the idea never became a reality and no book appeared.

Presented with the "Huddersfield Examiner," Saturday, January 7, 1893.

MR. WILLIAM SUMMERS.

Born November 4, 1853.   Died January 1, 1893.

(From a copyright photograph by Mr. J. E. Shaw, Huddersfield.)

An obituary recording William's death in India on 1 January 1893 appeared in the
Huddersfield Examiner.

William is remembered in this inscription on his parents' tombstone:

> Of a gentle and beneficent character,
> unsullied by intolerance or envy,
> he steadfastly devoted himself to
> the pursuit of the public good.

John

John, the third son, born on 21 January 1857, was the solid one of the family, the stolid one. When James, the eldest, was sent on a long sea voyage for the sake of his health, it was John who was brought from Owens College straight into the business. He remained there all his life.

James went to America to learn about the iron and steel business, while John, aged sixteen, stayed behind to learn about nail making. His brother William, who was nineteen, was much too busy studying the classics.

John started his day like the rest of the workers, at six o'clock in the morning. He was hard-working, conscientious and unimaginative. When Harry, the seventh son, filled with ideas for expansion and change, came into the business, it was always John who advised caution. Harry once said of him, 'He never dreamt of the realms which lay in front of him, waiting to be captured.' John was content to be regarded as a skilled nail maker.

When he was twenty-four John married a local girl called Ada. Another tea party was held in the Mechanics Institute to celebrate their marriage and all the works people were invited. Six hundred and twenty-two sat down to tea, and Jabez Pagden proposed the health of the young couple. Old Jabez recalled the days before John was born when he could count on his fingers the number of people employed at Summers. He told John that if his father had been there that evening, 'he would have felt a glow of honest pride in the respected position now occupied by his sons.'

John and Ada made their home in a shiny red brick house in Stalybridge, called Inglewood. From here John could walk to the works every day. Over the years they had four children, two boys and two girls. Theirs was a relaxed home, enjoyed by nephews and nieces as well as their own children. Especially remembered were Aunt Ada's gingerbread biscuits, the big attic full of junk and the swing hanging from the main beam where the children were let loose on rainy days.

In August 1903, the family were on holiday at St Ives in Cornwall. Their sons Jack, now aged nineteen, and Gerald, seventeen, spent much of their time swimming and Jack became very keen on diving.

The boys were sharing a bedroom in their hotel and before they went to sleep one warm night, Jack pulled down the sash window to get some air. Gerald woke in the night to see Jack climbing out of the window. He called to him to come back, but there was no answer as Jack disappeared through the window. Gerald ran downstairs with someone from the next bedroom. They found Jack lying on the ground, seriously injured. He never recovered consciousness and died later that night.

An inquest was held and it was concluded that Jack had been walking in his sleep. He had done it before as a small boy. The family thought that he must have been dreaming that he was diving, for it had been very much on his mind during the past few days and he had talked about it a great deal.

Whatever the reason for his death, John and Ada were heartbroken. They mourned their nineteen-year-old son. Then they buried their grief by devoting themselves to family and friends, and to the local community.

On their silver wedding anniversary John and Ada gave a thousand pounds to the local hospital, Ashton General. Ada was responsible for a special wing being built, primarily for the employees of the Globe Iron Works. She named

In 1919 Ada became the first lady mayor of Stalybridge.

it Summers Wing. Casualties at the works were rushed through the streets by a trolley relay team, two men at a time pushing the trolley while relief men ran alongside, waiting their turn to take over on the trolley.

Ada spent much of her time visiting the sick in hospital, and one patient recorded his gratitude:

> She was so generous, so practical in everything she tried to do to make life brighter for everyone. I should think everybody went to her with their troubles. Those were the days when 'recommends' were necessary for a bed in hospital, and those in need of a spell of convalescence needed a permit. Mrs Summers, above all, was the powerful influence who could bring this about.

John never really got over the death of his eldest son and he died on 20 May 1910, at the age of fifty-three. In his last years he was greatly respected at the works where he was called 'The Governor'. At his death this tribute was paid to him: 'Some men can ill be spared.'

Ada carried on with her good works, sitting on various committees and eventually in 1919 when she was in her sixties, she became the first lady mayor in Stalybridge. She held office for three years. All her life she remained in the town, a well-known character, described by one townsman as: 'easily recognisable in clerical grey walking as erect and as commandingly as a guardsman'.

Alfred

Alfred, born on 9 February 1861, was the fifth son, and the sportsman of the family. He was not just good at games, he excelled at them. When he was twelve he won a silver medal for athletics, and that was to be the first of many prizes and trophies for running and jumping.

At the Stalybridge Amateur Athletic Festival in July 1880, attended by over three hundred athletes, Alfred won a number of prizes. His cash prizes amounted to £13, and he handed the money back to his club to be used for cricket equipment.

The next year when he was twenty, he took part in the Athletic Meeting of Huddersfield and Widnes and won the championship medal for the long jump with a jump of twenty-two feet ten inches. He played cricket and football and rugby, all at club level, and was also good at billiards.

Alfred was a golden boy, fit, athletic and handsome, cheerful and popular with everyone, especially the girls. His younger brother Harry was quite jealous.

Alfred followed the pattern set by his brothers through school at Alderley Edge and Owens College, Manchester, but did not stay long enough to get a degree. He seized every opportunity to travel, and when he was twenty-three, he went to Canada and America as a member of the British Association. Two years later he went off to Egypt, Palestine and Greece in the company of brother William.

Alfred joined his brothers in the family business, but here he was no threat to young Harry. He was much more interested in what he did after work than what he did during working hours. Not that he was idle, but sport meant a lot to him and he was interested in politics and public affairs too.

On 26 October 1887, Alfred left the works in the middle of the morning and made for the railway station. Mr Gladstone was on his way home to Hawarden and his train was due to make a stop, so that the Prime Minister might address the people. Alfred wanted to hear what Mr Gladstone had to say, so he joined a crowd of two hundred or so on the platform. The Prime Minister spoke from the door of his carriage and then the train departed to loud cheers. Alfred lingered, first to congratulate Councillor Thorpe on his successful address to the Prime Minister, and then to pass the time of day with Canon Carroll.

By now it was almost lunchtime so Alfred set off to walk home to

A family group in about 1882, (left to right) Harry, Mary, William, Alfred, Frank, James and Walter.

Sunnyside. It was a long way round by road so he went along the railway line. This was strictly forbidden by the railway company, but all the Summers did it. Their father, John, had made a gate from the garden on to the railway line precisely for that purpose.

As Alfred walked along the track, his head filled with Mr Gladstone's rhetoric, the twelve twenty-five Stalybridge to Stockport train was just leaving the station, travelling tender first. It gathered speed slowly. The fireman suddenly spotted Alfred on the line ahead. The train whistled but Alfred did not appear to hear. He was still in the middle of the track when the train struck him and dragged him along the line. When it finally came to a halt, Alfred was dead. He was twenty-six.

Alfred's body was taken to the family home where the inquest was held. Harry Widdop, who was employed at the station to take train numbers, was only fifty yards away and had seen what had happened. He was asked:

'Did you see what injuries he had received?'

'He did not appear to have any, only his lower jaw was almost broken off.'

'His hat was knocked off, I suppose?'

It was suggested that a nearby goods train, blowing off steam, could have prevented Alfred from hearing the oncoming train. But most people in the town were convinced that he had failed to hear the train because his mind was preoccupied with Mr Gladstone's words.

The Liberals had planned a meeting in the town that night at which Alfred was to have taken the chair. They cancelled it and went round the town, putting up black-edged posters to tell everyone the tragic news.

Walter

Walter, the sixth son, born on 8 February 1863, was close in years to Harry who was born two years later, and equally close in confidence. Walter was the second boy in the family to bear that name. The fifth son to be born to John and Mary Summers had been christened Walter but he died in March 1863 when he was four, and the new baby who had been born the previous month was thereupon given the name of Walter.

He followed his brothers through school and Owens College and then, like William, he became a barrister. Again like William he did not practise at the Bar, but joined his brothers in the family business. In the 1890s however, when times were lean in the works, he went off to Ireland to manage the estate belonging to his brother-in-law, Abel Buckley, at Galtee Castle.

Walter's family life was not happy for long. His wife left him soon after the end of the First World War: his son, as a member of the family put it, 'turned out to be no good and died somewhere in South America': his daughter married a soldier who was killed in an air crash early in the Second World War.

But every month, without fail, Walter turned up at brother Harry's house for the Summers' board meeting, along with brother Frank. After the business had been concluded, the evening would be spent in playing bridge, and at such times Harry's son Richard was roped in to make up the fourth hand. He remembered, 'It was always instructive and amusing to play bridge with them. Bridge-playing seemed to bring out the greatest amount of acrimony possible and all three of them were very blunt in their criticism of the play of others.'

Walter spoke his mind bluntly at the board meetings too, but not harshly, and he always ended up supporting Harry. The two remained close through-out their lives and over the years Harry would often turn to Walter for sound, unbiased advice on business matters and personal affairs.

Walter carried his loyalty through to the next generation, when it was Richard's turn to lead the Summers' team, and sometimes he proved a useful buffer between father and son. Walter and Harry were the only two brothers to live beyond the allotted span of three score years and ten, and Walter was still on the Summers' board of directors when he died in May 1944.

Frank

Frank was the eighth and last of the Summers boys. He was born on 22 November 1868 and christened Frank Bright Summers, after the political hero of his father's youth. He grew up to like hunting, shooting and fishing and the good things of life. He was, said Harry, 'hail fellow, well met to all'.

Frank joined the family firm but saw no point in worrying his head about business matters when they were obviously in such capable hands. After all, his brothers had looked after him for as long as he could remember. He had been only two when his mother died and he was an orphan at seven.

Frank did not spend many years in the works and those that he did 'were not serious' in Harry's judgement. He kept his seat on the board but moved down to Hampshire and lived there in style with his wife and three surviving children, Billy, Phyllis and Spencer. Billy was killed in the Royal Flying Corps in the First World War, Phyllis married and moved out of the Summers' scene, but Spencer, born 27 October 1902, was destined to play a large part in the family fortunes of the next generation.

Meanwhile Frank continued to enjoy life; money had come to him easily and he parted with it just as easily. Reminiscing over the years, Harry said of him, 'Parsimony and frugality had no place in his nature.' But his generosity overflowed beyond family bounds and, like other members of his family, he gave to the local hospital and to those less well placed in his community.

For Frank it was a full life and a merry one but not a long one. He died on 27 January 1926 in his fifty-eighth year, succumbing to pneumonia following an operation for a perforated ulcer.

Mary

Mary, born on 2 October 1870, was the baby of the family. By now James, the eldest, was twenty-one: as first-born he had been given his mother's maiden name of Woolley and Mary, the last born, was also given her mother's family name. When she was only a month old her mother, worn out by years of child-bearing, died leaving her new baby daughter and younger sons to be reared by Nanny Walker and sister Hannah, who was almost twenty.

Within five years Hannah escaped from the beck and call of all her younger siblings into the responsibilities of her own marriage and household, and this was the first of repeated leavings throughout Mary's young life. Her father died when she was nine and afterwards her brothers, one by one, left the family home for their own marriages.

Mary's life does not enter the Summers' story, and her marriage in June 1896, to Doctor Percy Withers of Altrincham, is of interest only for the marked contrast with that of sister Hannah's twenty-one years earlier. This time the Summers family excelled in joyous celebration and generous hospitality, and every detail of the occasion was meticulously recorded by the *Stalybridge Reporter*.

The bride was dressed in heavy ivory satin trimmed with deep Irish lace and attended by four little Summers bridesmaids, all nieces, in pink satin trimmed with white pleated chiffon, and wearing white straw hats trimmed with pink gauze and white poppies. The bridal train was, in the *Reporter*'s words, 'borne in courtly guise by a tiny page boy gorgeously arrayed in white satin in antique costume'. This young page was Harry's four-year-old son.

All the brothers were present, accompanied by their wives, each dressed to outshine the others and to be a credit to the Summers name. The *Stalybridge Reporter* loved it; satin and silk, embroidered lace and fine feathers, not a stitch was missed in their coverage of the wedding. It would seem that Hannah, in white silk brocaded with heliotrope-coloured flowers, bodice trimmed with jewelled net and bonnet of roses, at last made up for her own quiet wedding. She gave Mary all she could wish, from her bridal gown to a fine reception at Ryecroft Hall, her servants decked out in new dresses in honour of the occasion.

When the day was over, the bride and groom left for their honeymoon in Scotland, where no doubt they hoped to try out her gift to him of salmon rod and tackle. Then it was home to Altrincham, where many wedding presents waited to remind Mary of her family back in Stalybridge.

THREE

The Seventh Son

Harry

Henry Hall Summers was the seventh son born to John and Mary. He arrived on 25 January 1865. Two boys had died in infancy so there were nine children all told to fill two of the cottages adjoining the Sandy Vale Iron Works. In the third cottage lived Jabez Pagden, the works manager. Jabez had two sons who joined him to work for Summers as soon as they were old enough to leave school.

Before Harry reached his fifth birthday his mother had died, on 2 November 1870, a month after the birth of her eleventh child. Nanny Walker, who had joined the family when Harry was born, took charge of brothers and sisters growing up together.

Nanny Walker was a widow without children; her husband had been employed in the Summers nail works. She moved into the Summers household and when Mary Summers died, Nanny Walker adopted the motherless children as her own. She kept alive the memory of their mother, telling her charges that their mother had been 'the most angelic person that ever walked on the earth. She would have gone through fire and water' for any one of them.

Much later Harry described Nanny Walker: 'Her admiration of them [his parents] amounted to worship without any discrimination between one or the other. She was a real pious early Victorian, most conscientious in everything she did.'

From what members of his family told him, Harry knew that his mother had spent her spare time in helping the poor and visiting the sick. Many in need or distress found their way to her door.

Room was found in the evening too, for old Mr Summers, Harry's grandfather. He came from his cottage nearby and supped his beer, sitting in his wooden upright armchair, which was always known as Grandfather's chair, and was seen home safely at bedtime by Harry's older brothers. He lived to be eighty-six. Harry remembered that he was buried in a nice pair of socks belonging to their father.

Harry grew up in the shadow of his father's works, within sight and sound and smell of the nail machines daily pounding away, cutting long red-hot nails. He could walk through his back yard straight into the works yard, and the first thing in view was a large nail machine under a lean-to shed. Across the road lived some of the Summers employees in Summers Street and Summers

Yard. Everyone with whom he came into contact in his early years was Summers born or Summers trained.

There were so many sons to carry on the family name, yet it was young Harry in particular who attracted the attention of one of his father's friends. A family story relates how this wealthy bachelor, who had made his money in the iron trade, offered John Summers £10,000 for Harry to become his son and heir, for as he told John, 'You have plenty of children and I have none.' The bargain was not concluded and Harry remained at home, under his father's guiding hand.

Looking back to his childhood in later life, Harry remembered being given very good fatherly advice, 'I must choose my friends well and always keep out of bad company, always be strictly upright and honest in all my dealings.' When the advice was forgotten, sterner measures were taken, as on the day when Harry stole a plum from a costermonger's barrow – 'just a boyish prank without any evil intention, but someone saw me and reported it to my father and I got a good whipping for it.'

Sunday was a day of rest and worship. John Summers did not often go to church himself but he made sure that his children, armed with hymn books and Bibles, went regularly, walking the mile or so to the Congregational Church. He had removed them from the parish church after one particular sermon had displeased him. The object of the exercise was for all to see that John Summers was a Godfearing man, and his family a pious one, even if he did prefer the stirring Liberal rhetoric of John Bright of Rochdale.

The Summers fortunes were steadily rising and, when Harry was seven, the family moved to Sunnyside, opposite Whitelands Twill Mill. It was a large stone mansion typical of the Victorian period with large entertaining rooms, library and morning room, five airy bedrooms one of which held three beds for the three youngest boys; but only one bathroom with a marble bath, located in the servants' quarters where there were two small bedrooms for the maids and the housekeeper's sitting room. Outside there was ground enough to stable three horses and carriages. Life was very comfortable for them all, but when Harry was only eleven, his father died.

Sister Hannah, who might have provided a warm loving centre for the young ones, had already left home to marry Abel Buckley, the wealthy mayor of Stalybridge. Harry could not have grieved at her going, for she was always more given to scoldings than cuddles, putting cleanliness before kindliness. Harry remembered one evening when he had made something in wood in his father's workshop. He brought it to show his father who was sitting with Hannah. She cried out, 'Look what a mess he has made of his clothes.' Father answered sharply, 'Never mind that, just look what he has made.'

The time came for young Harry to go to boarding school as his brothers had before him. He was never the scholar that William had been nor a sportsman like Alfred, but he was clever with his hands and soon mastered the tools of the school workshop. He was useful to the headmaster, Mr Wood, doing odd jobs around the school, but Harry smarted at the advantage he felt was being taken of him.

From Lindow Grove School he was sent for a year to Malvern School and then back on home ground to Owens College, Manchester, to follow the paths trodden by his brothers. But Harry was no academic and after only a year he left to earn his living.

His first job was in an engineering works in Gorton. Here he learnt the trade, starting in the pattern shop and moving through the other departments. After this, he looked around for something with more bite.

This was the early 1880s and fortunes were not being made as easily as they had been over the previous twenty years. Then, Britain's policy of *laissez-faire* had meant unrestricted trade with Europe, America and the Empire and our quality and cheapness of production had been far ahead of foreign competition. On the seas, sailing ships were gradually giving way to steam. The first iron hulls had been built in 1860 and within ten years there were more steamships under construction than sail.

Harry's father had moved into the iron trade at the beginning of the 1860s, using the wrought-iron puddling process for ironmaking, and the handrolling mills that had been invented at the turn of the century. He had turned out over one hundred tons of iron plates every week and sold them to small boiler shops in the district. Alongside his rolling mill and furnace he had run his nail shop.

The plate mill did not long survive John Summers' death in 1876. With the Siemens' Open Hearth Process, steel began to take the place of iron and the local boiler makers went out of existence one by one.

The problem now was to find a finished product to which the forge output could be diverted. Sheetrolling for nail production seemed to be the answer, but it was a costly operation and the plant was working very much under capacity. It was capable of between 300 and 400 tons weekly and the nail works were only using about 60 tons a week, and had small outside sales. In Harry's words, 'It was an ill-conceived fiasco . . . I don't remember whose misguided judgement was responsible for it.'

James and William, with brother-in-law Abel, were running the works. Brother John, a less ambitious man, was content to leave money matters to them and get on with the work of nailmaking, at which he was skilled. He was helped by brother Alfred.

Trade nationally was slow and manufacturers and industrialists were in a trough. The policy of free trade had been allowed too much freedom and now there was no protective shelter in subsidies as foreign competition grew. Industries across the country were cautious, unwilling to invest in new machinery and disinclined to take on more workers.

There was a similar mood in the Summers works in 1886. The Globe Iron Works had remained open and managed to avoid laying off any hands, but capital resources were being drawn on. The brothers considered there was no future for Harry in the family business. They suggested that now that he was twenty-one, he should take his share of the family estate left him in his father's will – it amounted to around £10,000 – and try his luck abroad. The idea did not appeal to Harry so, taking only a few hundred pounds, he tried his hand first at coal merchanting and then at the production of enamelled signs, both without much success.

Then, in the autumn of 1887, Alfred met his death on the railway line within sight of home and the family had to adjust to his loss. William was a busy and ambitious MP with limited time to spare for the making of iron. Abel had so many commercial ventures to occupy him as well as dabbling in politics that he could not be expected to give any more time to a business that, after all, was not in his blood.

There were, of course, managers at the works, Jabez Pagden in the nail shop, Trevelyan Sharp in the iron works, who were good men, but since John's death the business had lacked a leader with the courage to back his intuition and the drive to see it carried through.

Meanwhile, in his private ventures Harry had lost a few hundred pounds and gained some valuable experience. In May 1889, aged twenty-four, he married Minnie Gertrude Brattan, the daughter of a Birkenhead architect, and they set up home at Greenfield House, near Saddleworth, surrounded by moorland and hills. The house lay in the deep Chew Valley, almost at the meeting of four counties, Lancashire, Yorkshire, Derbyshire and Cheshire. Behind, the hills rose steeply to the two reservoirs of Dove Stone and Yeomen Hey that supplied water to Ashton, Dukinfield and Oldham. There was a third tiny reservoir, called Greenfield Reservoir, and above it, the Pennines stretched upwards into Yorkshire.

No doubt Harry came to know the house from visiting his sister Hannah and her wealthy husband Abel at Ashway Gap, the shooting lodge which they had owned for the past ten years. Greenfield House was only a step away from Ashway Gap, close by the road that led to Huddersfield, a road that had become familiar to them all since William had been voted to Westminster as Liberal MP for the town in 1886.

The brothers felt that it was not a good idea for Harry to be at a loose end and suggested that he had better come into the works. Perhaps his position as a newly married man and a man of property made him a more reliable proposition in their eyes. Perhaps, too, Harry was more ready to settle into the family firm than he had appeared to be a few years earlier.

Despite the daily five-mile journey into Stalybridge, Harry decided that this was the road he wanted to take and each day he drove himself to the works in

Minnie married Harry on 14 May 1889.

his pony and trap. At weekends the pony was used to pull the grass cutter over the garden lawns that covered nearly two acres.

On 11 December 1889, an account was opened with the District Bank of Stalybridge for the new partnership. All were Summers men – James, John, William, Walter, Harry and Frank. From the moment Harry stepped into the firm, he made his presence felt.

The demand for nails had dropped and the Globe Iron Works was working to only half its capacity. Harry saw that they must change direction. At his behest and in spite of John's protests at the size of the overdraft they would have to carry, the brothers decided to move into the production of iron sheet bars, rolled in long lengths.

The Minute Book of the District Bank recorded for 13 January 1890, 'A Mr James reported that some £10,000 would be expended in extending the Works.'

On 17 March further minutes read:

Mr J. W. Summers called about wanting more money. They are now £11,000 overdrawn and they require some more, probably £20,000 . . . He says their capital is £60,000 or £70,000. They are extending their works at a cost of £10,000 and hope to make a start with the new part on June 1st.

67

> They are at present putting into stock puddle bars to the amount of £1500 a month. These will be worked up into rod iron by the new works and they have now £10,000 in surplus stock and will have expended £10,000 in the new works.

Three rolling mills, driven by a steam engine, were erected. They worked well and three more mills were placed on the other side of the steam engine. Here, for the first time in this country, iron sheet bars were being rolled in long lengths.

After leaving the hot mill, the sheets were put through an annealing furnace to restore properties lost in the rolling process and sold as 'black sheets'.

Harry had been pressing all the time for the need to move into the galvanising trade but the others, especially John, were against it, pointing out that it was highly speculative, and failures and bad debts were not uncommon. They were also afraid that, by diversifying, they would lose their black sheet customers. But Harry chafed at being dependent on others' business acumen. He argued with John, 'I cannot imagine why we are rolling sheets and selling them comparatively cheaply to some people in Liverpool who galvanise them and sell them at a very much higher price.' John retorted, 'We are all right as we are.'

Harry kept up the pressure and at last, in 1894, it was agreed to erect one experimental galvanising pot on a vacant spot at the end of the sheet mills. It lay there idle for a number of months while Harry continued doing the rounds of the galvanising firms, touting for orders for their black sheets.

Then came a day when he was sent by James to Liverpool to see what he could pick up in the way of business. He got nothing although he pressed hard, threatening at one firm to move into their trade if he did not get an order. The response was nil, so Harry acted. He telephoned through to the works with the instructions, 'Start up the pot at once.'

It did not take long to convince the brothers that Harry's policy was the right one. Land was bought on the other side of the river, a bridge thrown across from the sheet mill bay and, in Harry's words, 'we never looked back'. They began to import iron bars from America for rolling into sheets, which meant higher productivity and better quality.

Soon there were six pots working. Sheets that were not sold as black sheets were either pickled or galvanised. The first method involved immersing the sheets in a pickling tank, in which scale and foreign matter were removed by acid. The acid was brought in carboys by canals but the trouble of handling them, the breakage and cost of transport, led the brothers to put up a condensing tower and saltcake furnace and the acid was taken directly to the pots in glass pipes.

The second process of galvanising involved coating the sheets with a protective zinc cover. Corrugating was yet another activity, but the manufacture of cut nails was still their main production.

Harry forecast that profits would rise to £100,000 in a year. John thought he was mad to entertain such an idea. Brother-in-law Abel summed up the situation neatly, ''Arry has more sense in his little finger than the rest of the family in the whole of their bodies.'

All available land at Stalybridge, twenty-four acres, was now under production with thirteen rolling mills, galvanising pots and finishing equipment. Harry's restless energy was urging him to look beyond the confines of the Globe Iron Works. He had business contacts with the port of Liverpool and family connections in Birkenhead. Within easy reach of both lay the desolate marshlands of the Dee estuary.

On New Year's Day 1894, the Manchester Ship Canal was officially declared open and in May the Queen gave her personal blessing to this daring and imaginative business venture by travelling north to Manchester for special ceremonies.

Apart from the obvious benefits to Manchester, Lancashire and the north, the new canal traffic had an effect on the port of Liverpool. Dock rates here became more competitive and services were improved. The same happened on the railways, as railway companies saw their freight trade going on the canal.

It was with this in mind that Harry went to explore six possible sites close to Birkenhead and Liverpool. He made his way to the boatyard at Connah's Quay in Flintshire and enquired for a boatman to take him out into the Dee estuary. Young Bill Butler was given the job in a home-made rowing boat. No rate was fixed for the job, but Harry told him not to worry; he would see he was all right however long it took.

Harry was rowed up the estuary in the direction of Chester, with the open sea at his back, and Welsh hills on his right. His eyes were directed to the land on the left which was the Sealand Marshes, bound on two sides by newly opened railway lines, the Dee & Birkenhead Railway and the Manchester, Sheffield & Lincoln Railway, the very line that served their interests at Stalybridge.

There were hundreds of acres of untamed grass-covered sand flats, home for thousands of wading birds and sea gulls. As the boat turned seawards, Harry could see that the sandy marshes extended towards Burton Point, and beyond were the sands of Parkgate, once a waterfront where travellers from eighteenth century Dublin had disembarked from the Irish packet boats. This service was forced to stop by the gradual silting up of the Dee estuary, which had been going on since the Middle Ages. There was still, however, an open channel down the middle of the Dee estuary that would give them access to the sea, and hence to the busy ports of Birkenhead and Liverpool.

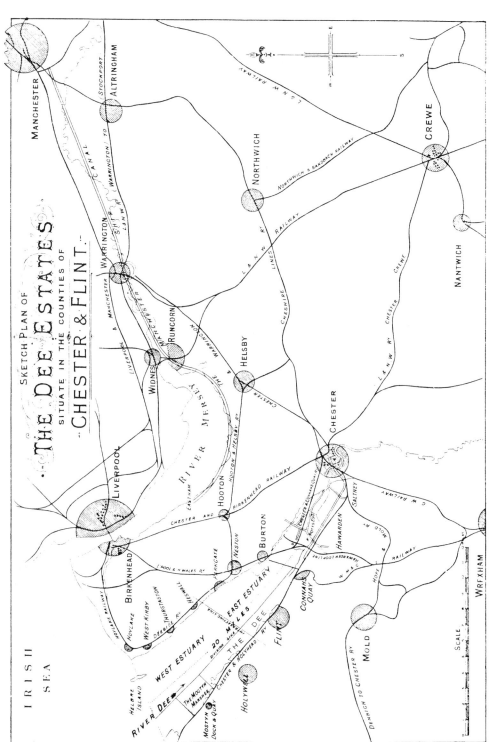

The Manchester Ship Canal opened in 1894.

It was low-lying, tide-washed land with few roads, but there were rail links, the open sea near at hand and plentiful supplies of water. On the Welsh side were collieries, brickworks and quarries. Moreover, the price per acre was low – tradition has it as low as one shilling an acre – and there was room in reclamation from the salt marshes for as much expansion as even Harry would need.

He returned to the boatyard at Connah's Quay and handed his young boatman half a crown. Then he went home to Stalybridge to report back to his brothers, well pleased with his prospecting.

On 1 November 1895 a meeting was held by the Manchester, Sheffield & Lincoln Railway Company and the minutes record: 'Summers & Sons of Stalybridge contemplate new iron works at Hawarden Bridge and have acquired some 40 acres by the Dee & Birkenhead Railway and the River Dee, also an option on 50 further acres. They have asked for a siding connexion to be laid at an estimated cost of £610.'

Within two weeks the news had reached the local papers. The *Chester Chronicle* of 16 November carried the story of the Dee Iron Works: 'A number of men are engaged discharging machinery required and a quantity of building material has also arrived so that in the course of a week or so building will be rapidly proceeded with.'

On 13 December at the next meeting of the Railway Co. there were further developments to note: 'Summers & Sons' activities involve acquisition of part of the golf links of Chester Golf Club. In consequence the platform near Wrexham junction built for the golf club had to be moved to a position near Chester junction at an estimated cost of £190.'

It was 1896 and time for a new agreement between the brothers. There were five of them, now that William had died of smallpox out in India.

At the time of this agreement, James, the eldest, was forty-seven and he and Edith were still living at Thomson Cross, Stalybridge; John was thirty-nine and he and Ada lived at Inglewood in Stalybridge. Walter, who was thirty-three, had just married on 6 February of this year and he and his new wife Dorothy were managing Abel's Irish estate in the county of Cork. Walter still had a large financial stake in the family firm, about £12,000, which had led the District Bank to look kindly on the overdraft of £2,000 that he had run up prior to his marriage. Harry was thirty-one and had recently moved with Minnie to Kelsall House, close by the Globe Iron Works. Frank had been married for four years to Constance and they had just set up home on the outskirts of Chester.

The agreement was for five years, or for 'as long as two or more survive'. Among the conditions were:

1. John and Harry must not reside at a greater distance than three miles from the Globe Works or Hawarden Bridge.

2. James, John, Harry and Frank were to give the whole of their attention and time.
3. Frank, the youngest at twenty-seven, would be on a fixed salary.
4. Cheques were to be signed by James, John and Harry.
5. Walter would remain as an adviser.

Harry and John remained in the Stalybridge area. Harry and Minnie were at Kelsall House with their two young children, Geoffrey and Maud. They had chosen the large stone house for its convenience to the Globe Works. A long footbridge built by the London & North Eastern Railway Co. led directly from the garden over the vast railway sidings to within fifty yards of the works gate.

Minnie Summers had exchanged the smells and smoke of the Greenfield woollen mill for the smells and smoke of the railways and iron works. Hardly an improvement but, of course, Harry no longer had the long journey every morning down the Huddersfield Road to the works. Harry's second son, Gordon, was born at Kelsall House on 15 September 1897.

In 1898 the firm became a limited company with a capital of £200,000.

Kelsall House, where Minnie and Harry lived within walking distance of the Globe Iron Works.

James, the eldest brother, was chairman and all the shares were held by the Summers family.

In that year, John Summers & Sons paid out £107,000 in wages and made 40,000 tons of galvanised sheet. The large bulk of this was made by the men at Hawarden Bridge, where there were now six steam driven sheet mills, galvanising pots, annealing furnaces and finishing equipment in operation.

Harry suggested to his brothers that he should go to look after the new project at Hawarden Bridge, but the idea was not popular. James and Frank were keen to take charge of the new works – in Harry's view the worst possible arrangement. Frank, however, had already bought a home near Chester and James was looking forward to moving his family to the area soon.

The general idea was that Stalybridge would remain the headquarters for the foreseeable future. Business at Hawarden Bridge was carried out in what had been the black and white fronted clubhouse of the Chester Golf Club, some of the golf links having been swallowed up by the new works. Off went James and Frank, taking with them a works manager, a galvanising manager, two engineers and a professional adviser.

John and Harry stayed behind to run the Globe Iron Works. A new office was built away from the noise and grime. Harry did not agree with this and told his brothers that this expenditure should never be used as an argument for keeping their headquarters at Stalybridge. He was well aware that their future lay near to the coast and, if they stayed land-locked, they would slip behind the other sheet-making firms in the country. They needed to import raw materials, and to export their steel sheets.

By 1900 there were twenty-one rolling mills at Hawarden Bridge Steel-works, in what was known to the workers as the Top Yard. Handrolling of sheets and hot dipped galvanising were their only activities.

Most of the sheet bars were imported from America, large quantities coming from the Carnegie Company. The steel bars came by rail from Pittsburgh to Baltimore, and hence were shipped to the port of Liverpool.

Regular supplies could not always be relied upon, and as the works expanded, the mills needed more and more bars. Like his father before him, Harry felt it unwise to be too dependent on others for basic supplies, and he urged his brothers to give Hawarden Bridge their own steel plant so that they could make at least a portion of their own steel bars.

In 1902 an open hearth steelmaking shop and a bar mill came into produc-tion to supply steel bars to the sheet mills. The No. 1 Steelworks had nine furnaces, each with a capacity of fifty tons. The Summers brothers, with Harry's driving force behind them, were continuing the process of vertical integration, begun by their father when he decided to make the nails that he needed for his clogs.

So now, for the first time, the steel sheets were home-made. The ingots of

steel, made on the premises, were rolled through the bar mill and the bars were
then rolled through a hand mill resembling an enormous mangle. As they
came out from between the two rollers, they were handled with tongs, for
they were red hot, and passed over the mill to handlers who were waiting to
put the sheets through the rollers again. This continued time and time again,
until the sheets were considered thin enough.

It took a crew of ten men to operate one hand mill driven by a steam engine.
The work was hot and dirty. The air was filled with dust and the smell of the
hot grease used to lubricate the rollers. All the operators wore stout trousers
and flannel shirts with sailcloth aprons or 'brats' to guard their legs, thick
socks and sturdy clogs. Around their necks hung sweat towels which they
clenched in their teeth, to catch the perspiration that ran down their faces.

In the galvanising sheds, dust and grease gave way to sulphuric acid fumes
that hung on the men's clothes and stained their teeth. The work was only for
the strong and the experienced.

With the building of the steelworks, production doubled to 83,000 tons and
the wage bill stood at £200,000. Harry was looking for ways to stimulate
management into even greater efforts. On 2 January 1904 he called a meeting
at the Stalybridge offices of all heads of departments and put before them a
profit-sharing scheme. John, Walter and Frank were there with James in the
chair.

Harry explained his scheme whereby each man would be paid a fixed salary,

Some of the steelworkers at the Hawarden Bridge Works.

and to this would be added a bonus in the form of a percentage of the profits. These were his main points:

> Look carefully at the men you have under you, give them every chance to help and advise you, don't get the idea that no one knows anything about your job but yourself. The secret to success is to surround yourself with able lieutenants. There is room for everyone to rise here . . . if you are the man for the job, you will step right into it. I hope it will never be necessary to go outside when there are vacancies to fill. I would rather have bread baked at home because I know what it's made of. We can do with any amount of rivalry, but there is no room here for jealousy.

Harry was seeking to reward and promote able, ambitious men into positions of trust within the family business, to fill the gaps that had been created by the passing years. The ideas were all Harry's, the brothers only had to go along with them.

James was still chairman, but at fifty-five years of age he was wanting to give more of his time to public affairs. He was about to accept the chairmanship of the local county council and, within a few years, would become the Liberal Member of Parliament for Flint Boroughs. He was, however, no high flier, and his constituency was just an extension of the family works. He addressed his political audience as he would a meeting of shareholders.

John had hoped to bring his elder son into the business, but just when his hopes were so near to realisation the boy had been killed in the sleep-walking accident of the previous summer.

Harry had three sons, all still at school. Geoffrey was the eldest, born on 2 September 1891. A daughter, Maud, had followed three years later on 23 December. These two had been born at Greenfield House, close to the Yorkshire moors. The second son, Henry Gordon, was born on 15 September 1897 at Kelsall House. He was Harry's namesake and favourite and most like him, so the family said.

A third son, Richard Felix, was born on 10 December 1902, shortly after Harry had moved his family away from the town centre of smoke and grime to The Priory, a large, grey, stone mansion. It stood well back from the main Stalybridge to Mottram road. The drive dipped steeply downhill, over a stream by way of a wooden bridge and then rose again, turning through trees to the main entrance of the house.

Even here the stonework was blackened by the smoky air, but the gardens were the children's delight. Railway lines were laid out for the boys' toy trains, tricycles were raced round the paths and there was a tennis court that became a marvellous place for Geoffrey to learn to drive a car – in those days it was a De Dion, capable of 20 mph maximum.

Minnie with Maud, Gordon and Geoffrey.

Indoors was Harry's workshop where he built and repaired grandfather clocks, a hobby that spilled over into the kitchen as he boiled the pieces from the old works in a copper pan on the kitchen range. Dead beetles, spiders and flies floated to the surface. The pieces could then be cleaned with paraffin and new parts made with a small hand lathe.

It was an idyllic family time that was abruptly ended by the death of Harry's wife on 9 December 1906, when she was thirty-eight years old. It was a month before Harry's forty-second birthday. He was left to bring up his children alone, as his father had been before him, in similar tragic circumstances.

It had been a cold damp foggy winter's day when Harry had insisted on driving into Manchester in the pony and trap. Although he had a car by this time, it never went very far without breaking down. While out on business, he was taken ill and his wife journeyed into Manchester in the brougham to bring him home.

Harry was suffering from pneumonia, a virus strain of the disease for which there was then no antidote. His wife nursed him through the attack and he recovered, but she caught the infection from him and within a few days she died.

Minnie and Harry's youngest child, Richard, born in 1902.

Minnie driving her pony and trap.

It was the day before Richard's fourth birthday and he remembered being sent to Uncle John's house to be out of the way. Geoffrey recalled that he had just started at Uppingham School.

Harry had not recovered sufficiently from his attack of pneumonia to attend his wife's funeral, which the local paper recorded sadly.

> On Wednesday, the dreariest and least kindly of December days, the remains of Mrs Summers were laid to their last rest in the churchyard at Mottram. How little while ago it seemed since her fingers were busy with leaf and flower decorating the old church for which she cared so much . . . Her life was lived not in the public gaze but in her home: not in the empty round of social amenities but in the full and satisfying obligations of family and friendship.

At the funeral service, in the crowded church at the top of the hill in Mottram, a violin solo, 'O Rest in the Lord' was played on her own Stradivarius by her music teacher, Mr Whitfield. Mrs Summers had lent her prized possession to him quite recently for a concert he gave in Ashton.

Her death was felt deeply by husband and children, who coped with their tragedy in different ways. Geoffrey was fifteen and desperately needed his mother's love and advice. 'I should have been a more useful person with her at my side,' he wrote later.

Geoffrey had shared his mother's great love of music and together they went to listen to the Hallé Orchestra at Manchester's Free Trade Hall. He learnt to play the piano, showing great promise, and loved to accompany his mother, who was a fine violinist. These shared experiences brought them close together. His boarding school was chosen for its high musical standards and perhaps, with his mother's support and encouragement, he could have made a name for himself on the professional platform.

Harry, however, had other plans for his eldest son. Although music was to remain Geoffrey's greatest interest, steel became his business.

Richard suffered the loss of his mother at roughly the same age as had his father before him, but there is no record of father and son finding comfort together in this generation. Richard seems to have been a quiet child, often ailing from childish complaints and spending much time on his own amusing himself. Feelings of insecurity, inferiority and timidity grew within him and had to be mastered when, as a man, he took on responsibilities for himself and others.

Maud was almost twelve when her mother died. It would be natural to expect that she might step into her mother's shoes and become the little mother to the men in the family, but Maud was away at boarding school and remained there until she went to a finishing school outside Paris.

Harry buried his grief by increased activity in the family business. What had been an absorbing job now became his whole life, to which he gave himself with single-minded dedication. He was not interested in making money, only in making more and better steel sheets than anyone else. He always wanted to plough back the money into the business, while brother John wanted to take his profits and invest outside the family firm. The two had many rows over this until the firm grew prosperous enough to keep John quiet.

When the Hawarden Bridge Works had opened in 1896 James and Frank had moved to take charge, leaving John and Harry in Stalybridge. John was content, the Globe Iron Works was a big enough world for him, but Harry sensed that their future lay near to the coast. At first, he visited once a week when, as he put it, 'the stage was carefully set for my coming'. If he stayed overnight, it was a case of camping in the makeshift wooden office with the office mice for company.

After each visit Harry came away discontented with the way things were being run. In his opinion, too many of the top men were taking too much time off to follow their own pursuits. James and Frank were not spending the hours at the works that they should, and in their absence, the managers were doing the same. Harry knew for a fact that two of the managers spent much of their time at a shoot that they shared on the coast.

James and Frank (centre) with managers and office staff at the Hawarden Bridge Works, including the office boys (on the ground).

The result was a drop in the quality of production, with many defective sheets that had to be sold off cheaply. Harry determined to find out what was going wrong, and after months of testing and sifting it was discovered that there were traces of arsenic in the ore that was being burnt in the chemical plant, which led to black spots developing on the galvanised sheets a few days after they had been dipped.

1906 saw the opening of an iron foundry at Hawarden Bridge. Now the rolls, brasses and general castings needed in the works could be home-made; one more step away from dependence on others. The following year more rolling mills were built.

John Summers & Sons Ltd was doing good business with the Argentine, selling galvanised sheets through agents in Buenos Aires. Lenders, a firm of exporters, mainly of cereals and hides, became their sole agents, and large quantities of galvanised sheets were shipped out through the port of Liverpool. However, Lenders ran into money difficulties and asked for a considerable loan. Harry felt he needed a trusted man to investigate on the spot on his behalf, and he sent out Mr Sharples to Buenos Aires.

Meanwhile, Harry investigated their financial state in this country and learnt that Summers stock had been pledged against Lenders overdrafts at a number of banks. Harry was advised to face the loss but he could not tolerate the thought of the rogues in Buenos Aires selling his stock and getting away with the profits.

Harry persuaded his bank and his board of directors that it was in their interests to take over Lenders in payment of their debt. In this he had the support of Henry Buckley, his friend and right-hand man in the firm, who spoke up for him; 'I don't like the situation at all . . . but I have such a high opinion of Mr Harry's judgement that I will not take the responsibility of saying that his policy must not be accepted.'

John Summers & Sons borrowed £250,000 from the bank, wound up Lenders and formed the Anglo-Argentine Iron Company (England) Ltd. Once all the obligations were cleared and anything profitable sold, the bank loan was down to £26,000 and in a few months this was cleared from current profits.

It was 1908 and production at Hawarden Bridge had become so much greater than at Stalybridge that it seemed obvious to move the company's headquarters to Shotton and to put Harry in charge there. His first action was to remove all the senior men who had been brought in by James and Frank. As he recalled many years later, 'I had what Hitler would describe as a purge.'

A totally new order was established; a new mill manager and engineer were appointed. One manager was sent to America to learn about the latest developments in the steel sheet industry; others were sent on holiday, only to find on their return that their posts had been filled.

The General Office, built in 1908, was designed by James France, Harry's architect friend.

A new, solid and imposing office building was erected on the banks of the Dee, aimed at impressing all who visited with the solid worth of John Summers & Sons. Profits now stood at £120,449, a rise from £40,163 in four years, and the subscribed capital in the firm had risen in the same period from £227,530 to £747,350.

Harry gave the job of designing the building to his great friend, the architect James France who was steeped in the Manchester Edwardian school of terracotta and shiny red brick, which explained why the finished work resembled the Midland Hotel in Manchester.

Harry also asked his friend to take charge of the modernisation plans for his new home at Cornist Hall near Flint, within the required three miles from the works, following Harry's original agreement with his brothers. All the latest modern conveniences were installed, including central heating and electric light. Harry had a passion for bathrooms and every bedroom at Cornist Hall had its own bathroom, a rare domestic luxury at the time. The ornate dining room was richly panelled with a heavy overmantel above the large fireplace in which Harry had carved the initials of his four children. While the alterations to the house were in progress, he lived in the smart new offices.

The children's nanny, Blanche Barton, moved with the family from The

Cornist Hall, Harry's new home near Flint, was modernised by James France.

Priory in Stalybridge to Cornist Hall, repeating the pattern of Harry's own childhood, when Nanny Walker had moved with the motherless children to their new home. Nanny Barton had her own sitting room, built over the front porch. Young Richard, now aged six, was her special charge and she indulged him as his mother would not have done. He was allowed to be over-fastidious in his eating habits and grew up to boast that he never ate anything that flew, swam or crawled.

Geoffrey, seventeen, Maud, fourteen, and Henry Gordon, eleven, were all away at boarding school and Richard was often alone with only Nanny Barton for company. When he looked back from adulthood, he remembered being very worried at nights if he felt that nanny was not in her sitting room, and if he heard anyone moving as he lay in bed he would call out, 'Are you taking care of me, Nanny?'

Richard was free, when not at school nearby, to roam through the large, echoing house and to play solitary games in the gardens. On wet days, he had great fun riding his tricycle and even his pedal car up and down the tiled passages all over the house. This can hardly have endeared him to the servants, but there were many of them at Cornist Hall and they were well looked after.

Harry began to spend more time in London, but he was always back at the weekends to hold the Saturday morning meeting at the works of all the managers, and to hear their report on the week's progress. When he did get home to Cornist Hall there was a fine workshop and a billiard room where he could relax from business pressures, often in the company of James France, an amusing man with a large ginger moustache.

Other friendships waxed and waned, but between Harry and James France it stood firm. The two were evenly matched at billiards and had many keenly fought games at weekends, when Mr France would often arrive on an enormous Red Indian motorcycle and sidecar of which he was tremendously proud. This was a powerful motorbike, imported from America – hence its name. It was a popular model.

Sometimes young Richard would watch their games of billiards, sitting on the leather fender round the fire. Looking back from adulthood, Richard remembered that they 'certainly had some amusing times . . . one day we were playing billiard fives, and his (Mr France's) false teeth fell out with a resounding noise on to the tiles of the fireplace.'

He would hear them playing late at night as shouts of derisive laughter reached him in his bedroom one floor above.

Serious work went on in the workshop at Cornist Hall which Harry equipped like a small factory and where he was joined by his good friend James France and his nephew, Kenneth Younghusband, who entered the family

Richard in 1910 when he was eight years old.

works in 1907 as an electrical engineer. When he was summoned to Cornist to help build the clocks, he dared not refuse. Not that he wanted to, because he loved working on the intricate timing mechanisms and his Uncle Harry was very good to him.

The three were locked away for hours on end, crafting the most beautiful grandfather clocks which kept perfect time to within one second per week. They showed the month, the day of the month and the day of the week on a four-year cycle, even having provision for leap year. The workmanship was superb; everything, apart from the face and hands, being built lovingly and patiently by the three men.

There was not much time for relaxation in the opening years of the new century. More rolling mills were needed to cope with demand and in 1911 the Marsh Mills were erected, with two engines driving the most up-to-date rolling mills in the country. By this time John Summers & Sons was employing over three thousand men, and the works had spread over two hundred and fifty acres of the Dee Marshes.

A nucleus of workmen had moved from the parent works at Stalybridge in 1896, and a band of workers from iron works in Staffordshire had come into the first mills, giving them the name of the Staffordshire Mills. This early workforce numbered about two hundred and fifty.

As the works expanded, men came from Birkenhead and Liverpool, from the Midlands and from North and South Wales. Welsh and English mingled harmoniously in and out of work. The works and the community grew together. The works grew on the north side of the Dee, but the workers lived on the other side of the river in the villages and small towns that stretched along the Flintshire side of the estuary, and scattered up and down the Welsh hills. Men came in daily from as far away as Wrexham, ten miles inland, and from Rhyl and Prestatyn on the Welsh coast. There was a good train service, although the wooden seats in the gas-lit carriages of those early trains made for hard, uncomfortable journeys.

As early as 1901 a group of managers in the works had banded together and formed their own building society to fund themselves. James became the first president of the Summers Permanent Benefit Building Society and the 1904 balance sheet showed a profit of seven shillings. Here was a way of helping the men to buy existing houses, although it did not address the whole problem.

There was an acute shortage of houses close to the works and Harry well knew the difficulties involved in bridging the miles between home and work. He had spent twelve years travelling between Stalybridge and Shotton, and only recently, in 1908, had bought his family home in Flintshire. It was, of course, family policy that John and Harry should live within three miles of the works, either at Stalybridge or Shotton.

Over the bridge of the Dee, from the works, stood the village of Shotton,

With the help of his friend, James France, and his nephew, Kenneth Younghusband, Harry built intricate and accurate grandfather clocks.

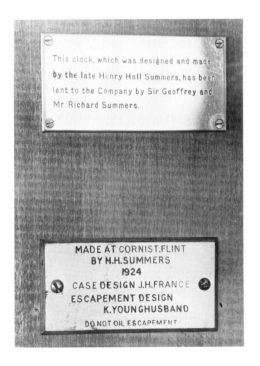

TELEGRAPHIC ADDRESSES:-
"SUMMERS, CONNAHS QUAY"
"SUMMERS, STALYBRIDGE"
"SPANGLER, LIVERPOOL"
"EISEN, MANCHESTER"

CODES USED:-
A.B.C. (5TH EDITION)
A.B.C. (4TH EDITION)
A.I. CODE
LIEBERS CODE

TELEPHONE NUMBERS:-
HAWARDEN BRIDGE, 535. CHESTER (4 WIRES)
STALYBRIDGE, 371.
LIVERPOOL, CENTRAL 6716 (3 WIRES)
MANCHESTER, 4956.

MANUFACTURERS OF
GALVANIZED, CORRUGATED & PLAIN SHEETS,
STEEL NAIL STRIPS & SHEETS, HOOPS, CUT NAILS, TACKS, &c.

LIVERPOOL OFFICE, 14 CHAPEL STREET,
MANCHESTER OFFICE, 33 BRAZENNOSE STREET,
GLOBE IRON WORKS, STALYBRIDGE.

HAWARDEN BRIDGE STEEL WORKS,
SHOTTON, FLINTSHIRE.

December 22nd, 190..

The extent of the works at Stalybridge and Shotton was displayed in the firm's letterheading.

and here a start was made on houses for the workers. The first were built in terraces at right angles to the main road that ran along the coast, parallel to the river. Summers' own building society provided mortgages and repayment was made direct from the workers' wages. On one of the railway arches at Hawarden, an unknown hand wrote, 'The wages of sin is death but the wages of Summers is starvation.' It was taken good-humouredly, for relations between management and men were good, but trouble was brewing among the rival unions in the works.

The trouble started in November 1909 and industrial strife raged on Deeside during the whole of the following year. It all began through what was known as the contract system.

Each rolling mill needed a crew of ten under the responsibility of one man, who employed and paid the others on a piecework system. The bossman or contractor was paid by the firm at so much a ton for the finished steel sheets. This meant that the contractor decided on the rates of pay and who should get what job. Favouritism was rife: a man who wanted promotion had to keep on the right side of the contractor.

The undermen began to join the Steel Smelters' Union, who approached the firm to abolish the contract system. Harry did not want to be directly involved, as he felt that it was an inter-union dispute which should be settled between the unions. He changed his mind, however, when an ultimatum was sent to him to abolish contractors, otherwise the undermen would strike. Harry made an agreement with the Smelters' deputation.

This brought out on strike the iron and steel workers, who refused to recognise the Smelters' Union and wanted to keep the system. The contractors did not want to pay the day-wage men a bonus, and argued that the best incentive to work was a plentiful supply of beer. Each shift had a beer carrier, employed at the rate of thirty shillings a week, which was seven shillings a week less than the rate for tradesmen, although men on piecework could earn much more.

Negotiations took place and agreement was reached, but Harry was trying to ride two horses at once. He made an agreement with the Smelters' deputation and, unknown to them, also made an agreement with the Ironworkers' Union. The strikers went back to work but the peace did not last. The undermen did not trust the union, who had spoken for the contractors, and insisted on recognition of their union. When it was not forthcoming, it was the turn of the smelters, fifteen hundred of them, to walk out on strike.

Harry tried to keep the works open with workers imported from Liverpool, but the steelworkers refused to work with blackleg labour. On 16 December, the *Flintshire Observer* carried the headlines, 'SHOTTON IRONWORKS MASTER'S DECISION'. The entire works closed down, with over three

The strike picket line on 12 February 1910.

The local constabulary at the time of the strike.

thousand men out of work, and shopkeepers in the district were seriously affected.

Pickets were posted on the gates and a large contingent of police from the surrounding areas and from as far afield as Manchester were drafted in to keep order and to guard the works. The local county council was meeting the bill, and it was felt that reconciliation must be tried before the long struggle dragged into the depths of winter.

The *Manchester Guardian* reported that from February to November the company had lost £60,000 because of the stoppage and the higher percentage of defective sheets that the outside labour had produced. Harry realised that something had to be done, and on 2 December 1910, he spoke directly to the workers at a meeting held in the works:

> Here is an opportunity of having a plain straight talk with you . . . I have been associated with this business for more than twenty years and until this trouble arose we were able to boast that in no single instance had we ever come into serious conflict with our employees . . .
>
> Gentlemen, I ask you is it right, is it fair that our works should be made the battleground for two trade unions to fight out their differences at our expense . . . There is work for every efficient man. With us efficiency will be the only standard of employment . . .
>
> I feel that I am entitled to ask for your assistance and my confidence in you is so great that I feel that I shall not ask in vain.

Harry did not ask in vain. Before the year was out, on 29 December 1910, the dispute ended. The three essentials for which the Steel Smelters' Union had fought were eventually established throughout the trade.

These were:

1. piecework basis of wages.
2. employment and payment of wages by the firm direct.
3. direct representation in respect of all matters affecting their wages and conditions of employment.

Not only were the workmen banding together to protect their interests, the foundry owners, steel manufacturers and galvanising merchants were doing the same. Harry once said of his brothers, 'although of different temperaments and at many times holding divergent views, we have always been able to smooth over our differences and work harmoniously together.'

Now Harry sought to inculcate those principles into the minds of his fellow iron masters. First came the Steel Sheet Trade Organisation regulating the selling of sheets, an idea thought up by Harry. Then the Galvanised Iron Association, with Harry as chairman, was formed. This led in 1913 to the Sheetmakers' Conference, with Harry again in the chair, and the formation of the Sheet Trade Board.

Not that Harry in any way neglected his own works while he took on, increasingly, commitments within the iron and steel industry. He was not a

In 1910 the works ambulance was driven by Thomas Williams.

big man but he had a strong, rasping voice and when he blew his nose the sound could be heard at least one block away. Perhaps because of this his workmen always knew when Mr 'Arry was about the place and everyone then seemed just slightly more efficient, even the managers to whom he was also Mr Harry, although to his sons and colleagues he was known as H.S.

Right in the middle of the troublesome strike John died of Bright's disease at the age of fifty-three. It was 20 May 1910. He was buried in Mottram Churchyard, alongside his son Jack. The Globe Works missed him greatly, as did the townspeople of Stalybridge, for apart from his constant presence at the works, John had been a JP and a good friend to the local hospital, giving generously both of his time and money.

Only three years later James died on the first day of January 1913, twenty years to the day after his brother William. James was sixty-three years old. As eldest son he had remained chairman of the firm, but for the past three years since becoming a full-time Member of Parliament, it was in name only.

James and Edith had lived in modest style at Emral Hall, Worthenbury, near Chester, a many-roomed seventeenth-century mansion which was the ancient seat of the Puleston family. Their only daughter was married to a captain in the Lincolnshire Regiment.

James had not been well for a number of months and had taken a trip to Egypt in the hope of improving his strength, but he returned to London to increasingly poor health. On his death he was brought home and buried in Worthenbury Churchyard.

In between the deaths of his two brothers, Harry suffered a severe body blow that grievously affected both him and his children. A day that began in joy and celebration ended in disaster. It was September 1912, and a house-party was in full swing at Cornist Hall to celebrate the twenty-first birthday of Harry's son, Geoffrey, on the second of the month. Geoffrey was now an undergraduate at Caius College, Cambridge, and most of the guests were his fellow-students.

On this particular evening, they all went off to a Liverpool theatre, among them Gordon, Geoffrey's fifteen-year-old brother, but not Richard who, at ten, was considered too young. On the way home the car carrying Gordon skidded off a bend in the road and hit a bank. Gordon was thrown out, his head hit a telegraph pole and he died instantly.

Harry's favourite son was dead, the one of whom he had expected great things and looked forward to succeeding him in the family firm; the one most like him. Harry wrote in his diary: 'At 11.45 p.m. our beloved Gordon was killed . . . we were all heartbroken that life so sweet, so promising should have been so tragically cut off.'

After this tragedy there was no way that Geoffrey could avoid the responsibilities that his father wished him, one day, to carry. He could forget his

Gordon on his motor bike in 1912.

boyhood ambitions of becoming a concert pianist. For Richard, Gordon's death meant the loss of a kind and patient older brother who was close enough in years to be a friend. Richard kept his happy memories:

> In the summer of 1912, we went to Criccieth and stayed at a house in the Marine Terrace. I remember that time fairly clearly because my brother, Gordon, had just got his motor bike, the Arno, and was allowed to take it with him. He used to take me on the carrier and allow me to help him to clean it, both of which I valued very highly.

After the tragedy Richard's feelings of insecurity and isolation deepened.

Harry, aged forty-seven, went on with the life he had constructed for himself after his wife's death six years earlier, but with renewed activity and even greater commitment to the business.

At the works Harry could finally manage affairs in exactly his own way. He had always felt curbed by John's over-cautious nature and restricted by James' narrow business outlook. Now he was uninhibited. His other brothers did not interfere.

Walter lived in Ireland and only put in a brief appearance at board meetings. At such times he met up with Frank who lived in the south of England, enjoying the country pursuits of hunting, fishing and shooting. Both brothers were only too willing for H.S. to shoulder full responsibility and to seize the business opportunities presented by war.

FOUR

The First War

1910 was the year of the smelters' strike. It was also the year of a wave of strikes that swept across the whole country, involving industries from cotton to coal. 1911 was no better with further strikes on the railways and in the cotton mills and at London, Manchester and Liverpool docks. In 1912 there was an almost total coal strike, paralysing industry and eventually settled by an Act of Parliament that allowed District Boards to fix minimum wages for coalmining. These strikes reflected not only the way that wages had lagged behind rising prices, but also the growing power of organised trade unions.

Once the smelters' strike was settled on 29 December 1910, there was peace at the works. Harry had always felt that 'the closer the bond between an employer and his workpeople, the better it must be for all concerned', and he firmly believed that conditions and earnings at his works were as good as anywhere in the iron and steel trade. Expansion at Summers continued, which was against the general trend in the country, and in 1911 the new Marsh Mills opened with twelve mills, soon increasing to nineteen.

The firm's policy of building houses for their workers must have contributed to the general mood of stability and loyalty within the works. An organisation called Sealand Tenants was set up so that it could benefit from government loans to help towards the cost of building houses. In July 1910, John Summers & Sons conveyed ten acres of their land to Sealand Tenants,

The river at Connah's Quay in about 1912.

H.S. standing outside the General Office.

followed the next year by a further sixteen acres, and in 1913 added still four more.

On this land the garden city of Sealand was built for Summers workers. It lay just behind the works on the same side of the river. Houses continued to be erected there until 1914, when the outbreak of the First World War brought house-building to a standstill. By this time, two hundred and eighty-three houses had been built but it was still a rural area surrounded by the green fields and hills on the Welsh side of the sandy estuary, and the Wirral countryside.

When H.S. became chairman after James' death on 1 January 1913, he took charge of a company with the most up-to-date equipment in the country, thanks mainly to his own initiative and zeal. The outbreak of the First World War in 1914 called for more steel sheets for trenches and Nissen huts, and the Government handed out money to enable firms to increase their steel capacity. Every effort was made at the Summers Works, and all the rolling mills were producing maximum output.

As the war with Germany dragged on from months into years, H.S. realised that the nation would need much larger supplies of steel than it was capable of producing at present. Shotton must expand immediately if advantage was to be taken of the demands for steel. Thousands of steel sheets were needed for making shells.

It was 1916 when H.S. decided to cut through bureaucratic red tape, for which he had never had much use. He travelled up to London and went straight to the Department of Trade. He was told that there were alternative schemes on offer to businessmen seeking to expand in order to help the war effort. He was given all the particulars and advised to go away and think about the schemes, then write to the Department when he had made up his mind.

H.S. asked when lunch was. 'One o'clock,' was the reply. 'Very well,' said H.S. 'I shall give you my answer before then.' He went straight to his London office, telephoned Shotton, and then made his decision.

The day was Wednesday, the time was 11 a.m. By lunchtime a deal had been struck and two days later the first sod of turf had been cut at Shotton. Railways were being laid to the newly marked-out site, and within twelve months of cutting the first sod, the first steel was made.

The new No.2 Steelworks and Bar Mill completely freed the firm from dependence on imported bars, an enviable position first inaugurated by H.S. as long ago as 1902, when he had urged his brothers to invest in No.1 Steelworks with ten furnaces. The new steelworks was equipped with eight open hearth furnaces, each with a capacity of 70–75 tons.

Other firms had undertaken expansion during the war years, but none with H.S.'s success. He was blessed with an energetic manager at Shotton, Bruce Gardner, who lived on the job from start to finish. His sound judgement and dedicated enthusiasm ensured success then and later when he reorganised the Shelton plant.

H.S. explained the opportunity that war had brought him like this:

> The scheme was simple. We had to find the money but we were allowed to deduct out of money payable to the revenue for Income Tax, Excess Profits Tax or any other taxes which might be imposed, up to two-thirds of the cost of the plant.
>
> The plant cost £900,000. Within eleven months we made steel and deducted the money as agreed, and within two years the transaction was closed. We had much more than enough profit to cover us and the plant remained on our books at £300,000.

Until the war the only woman working at Shotton Steelworks was the caretaker's wife, Mrs Clements. She kept a motherly eye on the young office boys and sold them cups of tea at lunchtime for a penny a cup. But the flow of men into the armed forces left gaps at all the office desks and women were brought in to do the clerical jobs.

Once in, the women stayed in the offices and canteens, but steelmaking itself was considered men's work and only for the strongest and fittest.

The war took its toll of Summers sons. John had already lost his son in the sleepwalking accident and Harry his favourite in the car crash. In 1916 James' only son Alfred was killed, leaving behind a young widow and a baby son. Alfred had been in the Royal Flying Corps, and so had Frank's eldest son Billy, who was killed in the same year. The promise for the future was being savagely cut down, but it was not entirely destroyed.

Geoffrey, Harry's eldest, had joined his father in the family business just when Harry had taken over the chairmanship, James having died on 1 January 1913. Geoffrey now carried the hopes not only of his father but of most of the Summers family. But was he the man for the job? He was a retiring, uncomplicated man who took life at face value and did not look for the complexities beneath. His greatest delight was to sit at his piano and quietly entertain himself.

He had ended his student days at Cambridge with a grumbling appendix, and when war came, he decided to have it out so that he would be fit to enlist. After the operation he suffered from digestive troubles and was found to have a stomach ulcer. This was medically treated and finally cured, but Geoffrey was not fit enough to qualify for active service, something he always regretted. He did get into the army and reached the rank of captain, but his service was confined to home ground and he was stationed not far from the family steelworks.

His sister Maud was doing her bit for the war effort as a member of a Red Cross ambulance crew in France. The social graces that she had acquired at her Parisian finishing school seemed of little use now, but she had learnt a little about the country and the language, which was an asset to her. While at her French school, she had made friends with another English girl whose home was in Kent. In the holidays Maud had brought Doris home with her to Cornist Hall, where Geoffrey fell in love with her and married her on 16 September 1915.

Geoffrey and Doris set up home in a small flat in New Brighton on the northern edge of the Wirral. After all, there was a war going on and this was not the time to be thinking of luxuries. In December 1916 a daughter, Anne, was born and two years later, on 1 October 1918, just before war ended, Geoffrey became the father of twin sons. After five years in uniform, Geoffrey, now twenty-seven, returned to the family works and gave his attention to making steel.

Geoffrey's marriage had perhaps made his father even more aware of his solitary state and the loneliness that he had endured since his lovely wife, Minnie, had died. Harry owned a very large, very beautiful home not far from his beloved steelworks. No expense had been spared in modernisation and furnishing, yet Harry spent more days in London than at Cornist Hall in Flintshire.

He had been alone for ten years. He had an eye for a pretty face and enjoyed feminine company but no one that he had yet met measured up to his dead

During the war, Maud worked as a member of a Red Cross ambulance team in France.

wife. Both Geoffrey and Richard believed that their father was searching for a lost ideal; Richard felt that his father swung violently from one extreme to another, that at first when he met someone she could do no wrong, but after a few years there was nothing bad enough that could be said. The same applied to men whose friendship did not last.

For many years Harry maintained a London home as a useful base from which to keep up with his business and social contacts. The picture is of a man confident and successful in his business sphere, looking for an affection and understanding in his personal life that eluded him. He was a member of various clubs and particularly liked the Liberal Club, where he could gossip with his cronies.

One evening a doctor-friend joined him for a night-cap and over drinks told him of a pretty girl who was currently his patient in a nursing home. She was a chorus girl called Marjorie Agnes Standish Thomson with a small part in *Charley's Aunt* and she had been taken ill with appendicitis after a performance.

Harry thought it seemed a good idea to pay her a visit and from the first moment he was completely captivated. After three visits they became engaged but Marjorie kept it a secret from the nurses and wore her engagement ring on a chain around her neck. Harry, middle-aged, squat and balding, could not have been her ideal choice, but he was rich and kind and Marjorie envisaged a marvellous life of pleasure and luxury.

Marjorie, the nineteen-year-old chorus girl whom Harry married in 1917.

She was nineteen, pretty and sweet-natured, full of high spirits and fun-loving. She was completely swept off her feet by Harry's generous gifts and powerful persuasion and they were married as soon as a licence could be obtained, in the Chapel Royal of the Savoy precinct. It was 13 January 1917, shortly before Harry's fifty-second birthday. Whether Marjorie's family approved of her hasty marriage is unknown – her father, a naval captain, was no doubt otherwise occupied at this time – but parental permission was obtained and her brother acted as her witness, while Harry was supported by his brother Frank.

The marriage was doomed from the start. Marjorie was closer in years and inclinations to Harry's sons, and once she was mistress of Cornist Hall she did not keep her side of the marriage contract. While Harry was in London during the working week, Marjorie's life became a round of pranks and parties. Young men danced attendance on her, the young officers from the army camp nearby came in droves, and Richard's friends made straight for Cornist in vacations. The combination of Marjorie's charms and the contents of the Cornist wine cellar were irresistible.

Harry asked little from his pretty gay wife but before long his patience gave out. He was forced to take notice of gossip as Marjorie threw discretion to the winds. Frank, present at the wedding, had predicted five years for the marriage. It actually lasted seven and two years later ended in divorce in 1926.

FIVE

The New Generation

In the immediate post-war years, Shotton was a success. The workforce had risen to 5,800 and the firm was the second largest producer of steel sheets in the country.

Although no longer dependent on steel bars from abroad, the works still needed outside sources for its raw materials of pig iron and coal. H.S. realised the strategic importance of securing these supplies.

In 1917 the Wolverhampton Corrugated Company at Ellesmere Port was acquired, which brought another twenty sheet mills into the Summers empire. In the same year the Castle Fire Brick Company at Buckley in Flintshire was purchased which solved the problem of a shortage in refractory materials for lining the furnaces.

In 1920 Shelton Iron & Steel & Coal Company at Stoke on Trent, which had surplus pig iron capacity just when this commodity was scarce, was bought, together with a couple of collieries owned by the company.

The end of the war brought an artificial period when prices rocketed. The years of hardship and deprivation were ended, or so it was thought, and everybody wanted more home comforts and a higher standard of living. The demand for steel was echoed in all industries and prices reached ridiculous heights. Steel sheet was up to £54 a ton. Summers was exporting 90 per cent of its output, nearly all galvanised, to countries as far away as India, Africa and South America.

The company had built up its own fleet of ships to ply between the works and the ocean-going ships at Liverpool. By the end of the war there were nineteen of these ships, known locally as the Beetle Fleet. They were neat, busy little ships that suited the narrow, tidal Dee channel perfectly. The steel sheets were loaded straight from the ships into the holds of the big ships tied up at the Liverpool docks.

It was a boom time, but short-lived. Many countries now began to make their own steel sheets, investing in home industries. This brought a higher standard of living to their own people, who no longer wanted galvanised sheets for roofing.

In 1925 the Argentine government imposed a substantial preferential duty on galvanised sheets and a small duty on black sheets, and a local firm started its own galvanising plant. Harry again, as in 1908, sent a trusted man out to the Argentine to investigate the situation. This time it was John Pagden, son of Jabez and an experienced works manager. Then Harry travelled out to Buenos Aires to see for himself and to set up a galvanising pot in Summers' own name. He quickly realised that it was going to be a very profitable venture and that

H.S. accompanied the Prince of Wales on his tour of the works on 13 June 1924.

Summers must press on and increase its output as quickly as possible.

Harry cabled details of the expenditure and the amount of capital outlay to his board at home. He wished to build an extensive galvanising plant and buy an existing warehouse, involving altogether the sum of £40,000. The reply came back: 'All the directors assembled at Shotton unanimously of opinion that your scheme is too costly. There will always be a prejudice against locally made sheets and in favour of imported ones. We advise move with caution. Do not buy any more property.'

Once again Harry's ambitious plans were being opposed. He replied that there was no prejudice against locally made sheets; imported ones were bought because the others were not available. The next cable was brief: 'We leave the matter in your hands.'

A new company was formed in Buenos Aires which took over all the assets of the old Anglo-Argentine Company. Its new title was the Anglo-Argentine Iron Co. Ltd. Buenos Aires. The company prospered and sales expanded so rapidly that pots were put down wherever there was room.

In Britain as the demand for galvanised and corrugated sheets was falling, there came an increasing demand from the motorcar trade for a better quality steel sheet. So, while traditional markets were being lost, experiments were going on to find a new and better way of producing steel. The time of transition begun in the mid 1920s lasted about ten years, and coincided with the world-wide period of overproduction followed by a slump in trade and an ensuing loss of confidence. At the end of this period steel sheets in this country were down to about £16 a ton.

In 1925 the Americans were the first to introduce the continuous rolling of steel strip. Before the First World War Henry Ford's company had developed an assembly line technique that enabled the company to mass produce cheap standardised cars, and the Americans were forging ahead in the motorcar trade, using steel when in this country we were still using aluminium or wood. The Americans were also ahead in steel furniture for offices, homes and kitchen equipment. It was only a matter of time before their methods and ideas crossed the Atlantic.

What of Harry's two sons in the immediate post-war years? Richard had been fourteen when his father had brought Marjorie home as his new bride. Nannie Barton left at once to live with her sister. She had been housekeeper and nanny to Richard since he was four years old, but she saw that times had changed and that big as Cornist was, it could not accommodate her and Marjorie.

In 1921 Richard left his Shrewsbury school and followed Geoffrey to Cambridge, choosing Clare College rather than Geoffrey's old college of Caius. Here life was made bearable by the acquisition of his first car, a Morris Cowley, soon exchanged for a sports model.

Thursday was early closing day in Cambridge. Shops and businesses came to a standstill at lunchtime and workers went home. This was the practice in the garage where Richard kept his car and, once the mechanics had left, there was space for him to move in. On those peaceful Thursday afternoons Richard would happily while away the hours adjusting, cleaning and polishing his car. After a few weeks he noticed another undergraduate doing the same on the other side of the garage. They swapped motoring gossip, struck up acquaintance, discovered a shared enthusiasm and became life-long friends. The man who came out from under the bonnet of his car to meet Richard was Neville Rollason.

Richard's idea had been to read economics, but his father had scotched that as being a complete waste of time. So Richard ended up doing one year of chemistry, one of geology and one of history. The last was chosen for the least number of lectures and, Richard hoped, a light work-load. Looking back much later to his student days Richard observed:

> In those days . . . nobody cared very much whether you worked or whether you did not. There were still a number of ex-officers from the army and navy there who had interrupted their University career to serve in the war; they were a pretty rowdy crowd and discipline was very lax with the result that I had an extremely pleasant three years.*

---

* Memories written down 28 April 1948.

He achieved the minimum amount of work and the maximum amount of motoring in his final year. He changed his car for a 30/98 Vauxhall blue four-seater and entrusted to Neville the job of driving it, brand new, from the Luton factory.

Then Richard was laid low with appendicitis, but once the offending appendix was removed, the time of convalescence was a great opportunity for motoring. He went off for a six weeks' tour of Switzerland.

It was May 1923, just about the time when Geoffrey was allowed to take three months off from the steel-works. Geoffrey was now on the board of directors but here was a welcome break from duty, and also from his ailing eight-year-old marriage. His twin sons were difficult children and nannies and governesses came and went with distressing regularity. Geoffrey had discovered the benefits of rockclimbing both for his physical wellbeing and for his mental relaxation when he had been recovering from his stomach ulcer in the war. It offered a means of escape from the harsh realities of life, and now he had the chance to join the Merton College Expedition to Spitzbergen.

Another member on this Arctic voyage was Sandy Irvine, Richard's best friend from Shrewsbury schooldays. Richard had often been home with Sandy and made friends with his sister Evelyn, who was a couple of years older than the boys and reading chemistry at Oxford. Sandy was equally at home at Cornist Hall and enjoyed the chance of flirting with Richard's fun-loving step-mother.

Sandy Irvine, who became Richard's schoolfriend at Shrewsbury.

Sandy and Geoffrey sailed for Norway, under the leadership of Noel Odell, their aim being to circumnavigate Northeastland, a large island off the north of Spitzbergen, only about 400 miles from the North Pole. They failed in their attempt because of ferociously packed ice, but it was a memorable time for Geoffrey. Their only companions were polar bear, reindeer, walrus and seals; the only noise came from glaciers sliding into the sea. Even the seabirds had less to say than round Llandudno Pier – or so it seemed to Geoffrey.

After three months of exhilarating physical endurance, they returned to civilisation and a welcome from the girls they had left behind them. Geoffrey's wife Doris, Harry's wife Marjorie, and another girl friend had decided it would be a marvellous lark to meet the men in Norway and celebrate their safe return.

While Geoffrey and Sandy were thus occupied in the summer of 1923, Richard was having fun in Switzerland, France and at home. He took his blue Vauxhall to the race tracks of France and England. He came second in his class in the Boulogne Speed Trials and second in speed trials at Shelsey Walsh, beaten only by Malcolm Campbell's racing Sunbeam.

He had one more term to complete at Cambridge to gain his degree because he had lost a term over his appendicitis. Before going up for the Michaelmas term he became engaged to Evelyn Irvine – and caused a family row.

Richard's friendship with Evelyn had blossomed into romance while Sandy was away, but now, back at Oxford, Sandy could not see his way to support his old school chum on his engagement to his sister. He wrote to Richard:

> I'm always your best and truest friend . . . Just think for one moment what I would be like if I had never met you – probably never seen town at all, certainly no theatre, no workshop, no fun with cars, no Brooklands, no priceless holidays in the Lakes. Dick, I'll never forget those two days last vac., the most enjoyable of any I can ever remember . . . but I think you are a fool . . . if it's of convenience . . . damn carelessness . . . To be quite serious I know that neither father will hear of it and none of the brothers . . . Have a good night's sleep, a cold bath, read your morning paper and think twice, then again.

On the same day Sandy wrote to his sister:

> I like him more than any man I've ever met – there isn't a kinder or more generous soul in all the world but you'll have to make a real man of him before I'll feel happy about it . . . oh E. it's all very upsetting . . . My only hope is that you let it keep for a bit and go wintersporting or do something where you meet a few more men.

Evelyn Irvine, to whom Richard became engaged in the summer of 1923.

Parents on both sides bore down on Richard with words of caution and advice, telling him to wait three months, twelve months. Evelyn's mother wrote quite explicitly,

> My dear Dick,
>   You and Evelyn have given me such a shock I really can't get over it. What are you thinking about? Fancy wanting to get engaged before you are twenty-one and to my daughter of all people . . . Are you quite sure that you will always love her better than the most beautiful record-breaking motorcar that ever could be invented? . . . I didn't think that either of you were anything but very good pals.

All this good family advice fell on deaf ears. Richard knew what he wanted, although not yet twenty-one. In many ways he was older than his years. From the time of his father's second marriage when he was fourteen, he had been thrown very much on to his own resources with no one to reassure him of his own worth. Now he had met a loving, dependable woman whom he loved and who, he knew, would be the companion that he desperately needed.

The next year, Sandy was included in the expedition to climb Everest. Odell, who had led the Spitzbergen team, had been impressed by Sandy's character and physique which, he felt, compensated for his lack of mountaineering experience. Sandy had rowed twice for Oxford, was magnificently fit as he had proved on the Spitzbergen trip when he had been one of the sledging team, and he had a mechanical aptitude that could be useful to the Everest team.

He said goodbye to Dick and Evelyn and set off for Everest in high spirits. Someone who was unable to say goodbye was Marjorie, Harry's pretty young wife. She had been straining at the marriage leash for some time, trying Harry's patience to the limits. Her decision to follow Sandy part of the way to Everest was just too much. When she returned to England it was not to Cornist Hall. She and Harry agreed to separate and divorce followed in 1926. Harry was generous in his settlement for her, as long as she kept to the arrangement that she stayed at least ten miles away from Cornist Hall.

Sandy Irvine lost his life on the final assault on Everest with Malory in June 1924. Richard was in London at the time, staying at the Metropole Hotel, on the way to Herne Bay where he was taking part in some speed trials. He remembered going down to hotel breakfast and stopping to buy a newspaper that carried the story that Sandy was missing on Everest. Richard packed up at once and went home. He and Evelyn needed each other more than ever now. As always, Evelyn gave him comfort and strength and the confidence to face the world and carry on. They were married on 21 April 1925.

As it had his father before him, marriage concentrated Richard's thoughts on joining the family firm. He and his new bride set up house close to the Shotton Steelworks. Their home looked out from the Wirral across the Dee marshes to the Shotton chimneys and the Welsh hills beyond.

Even though he was now a married man his father did not think he was old enough to make his own decisions:

> I do not think Richard ought to have bought a house for £10,000 without asking a word of advice from me. It is true that the money I have given him is entirely at his own disposal but at the same time, as it came from me and I am still here, I would have liked to have been consulted.

H.S. complained to Geoffrey, who now lived at Northop, across the Dee estuary from Richard and Evelyn.

The journey to the works from Richard's home was nine miles around the estuary, but he soon changed that. He built a private road directly across the marshes, a distance of four miles. Like his founding grandfather, Richard intended to live close to the job, although it may not have been enthusiasm for his employment that brought about the straight crossing from home to work.

The new road had two miles of dual track with a roundabout at the ends, the family's own miniature race track.

Many exciting duels were fought between this new generation of Summers in their latest motor cars. Richard still had his beloved Vauxhall from student days, as well as an Aston-Martin. Geoffrey raced against him in his Rolls-Royce Phantom. Cousin Spencer, Frank's youngest boy, drove a Lancia-Lamda. Neville Rollason came over with his Vauxhall, companion to Richard's. Even H.S. joined in sometimes with his Chrysler. The merits of each model were hotly disputed and formal records were kept as they put their cars through their paces.

There was not much time for fun and games. H.S. was spending most of his working week in London, but he was always at the works on Saturday morning to get a full progress report from his managers. Everyone was expected to be there, nothing was considered too important to be cancelled or postponed for these meetings.

Richard described the scene. 'H.S. was dictator with Mr Buckley a very able lieutenant with wise counsel'.

Henry Buckley was one of H.S.'s greatest admirers and strongest supporters. He had come to Stalybridge as an office boy and spent all his life with John Summers & Sons, now acting as managing director under H.S.'s chairmanship. He was only really happy at his office desk, helping to solve the innumerable problems which confronted him.

H.S. was now sixty years old, an age at which many men would be looking forward to taking life a little more easily, but that was not his attitude. Brother Frank, although three years his junior, retired from the board in 1925 and died the next year.

Hardly a day passed, wherever he was, when H.S. did not receive a telegrammed report from Mr Buckley at his office desk. On Sundays when he was at home he never missed going to the works. He would wander around, missing nothing, wanting to know exactly why a machine, a tool or a man was working in a different place from last time.

What was going on at the works dominated his thoughts and he was constantly spurring his sons to greater efforts and to more commitment to the family concern. He told Geoffrey one day, 'I feel I have taken on a great responsibility and my great desire is to feel that you and Dick can and will carry on.'

The years between the wars were critical times and there were weaknesses in the family management. A generation had been lost in the 1914–18 war. James' son and Frank's eldest had been killed, serving in the Royal Flying Corps. John and Harry had lost sons in terrible accidents.

The new generation had much to learn. Geoffrey was moving through the many departments of the steelworks, without much direction, trying to understand the technicalities of steelmaking. He got on well with the workers and enjoyed the human problems rather than the technical ones. In 1927, now almost thirty-six, he was sent to America to see how it was done there, as his Uncle James had been fifty-four years ago when he had been only twenty-four (that generation had come up against the real world much sooner).

Spencer, at the age of twenty-four, was learning the commercial side of the business. Richard at the same age was learning how to run the Castle Fire Brick Company, but he felt keenly his lack of technical knowledge. He wished that his responsibilities were more specific. There were many hours when he was at a loose end and spent the time tinkering with his car engine.

The traditional methods of steelmaking were being modified as new industries called for a new kind of steel sheet. Motorcar bodies and steel furniture needed more malleable sheets of finer surface quality and thinner gauge.

The firm had to keep up with developments and in 1928 the American Rolling Mill Company, who were experts at producing high grade sheets, joined with John Summers & Sons Ltd. for experiments in the improvement of hand mill techniques. Changes were made in the open hearth practice, specifications tightened and the rolling processes were modified. Electric motors were installed instead of steam engines to drive the mills.

By now Geoffrey was second-in-command to H.S. on the board of directors. An outsider, Reith Gray, introduced by Spencer, joined the family ranks. They had been students together at Cambridge and apprentices in ship building yards Swan Hunter on the Tyne. Reith Gray became plant manager of the new high grade sheet department. He was the complete professional, technically skilled and experienced, yet one of the men.

On 2 November 1928, Geoffrey sent all workers on the new production line a letter:

> This week marks the beginning of a new era in the history of our firm . . .
> This is a new trade – almost a new art that we are setting out to learn. Some
> of the sheets we hope to make will be different from – and better we hope –
> than any sheets yet made in Great Britain. Old methods and habits must be
> forgotten and new ones absorbed . . . You will have noticed the trouble
> and expense we have incurred to make the plant clean and attractive. Our
> finished product must be absolutely free from blemish . . . even a human
> hair on the cold rolls could so mark a sheet as to spoil it as a first grade
> product . . .
>
> Floor plates, mill housings, shears, furnaces etc. etc. will have to be kept
> scrupulously clean.

H.S. was critical of his son's priorities. Nearly a year later he was still remembering, 'I think if Geoffrey had control of the works, in two or three

Reith Gray joined Summers in 1928.

years we might have a nice place to look at but we should have no money.'

Old methods had to give way to new. Mistakes were made, left to multiply or to act as stumbling blocks in the smooth operation. The new young managers had not yet acquired the experience to guide their judgement or to realise the extent of their mistakes or the size of the losses.

The quest for a better quality steel was going on throughout the steel industry, and in the years between 1928 and 1937 there were many experiments at John Summers & Sons to improve their quality. There was a limit to what could be achieved by hand rolling and it was not an easy time to introduce new techniques when world demand was so uncertain.

The high grade sheet department, known in the Works as ARMCO after the initials of the American company, was placed under American management in order to solve the problems which the young English managers and directors could not master. The man sent over was called Hoover. He was given a free hand to make whatever alterations he thought necessary, a move which only added to the anxieties.

Hoover was a fast worker. He sought to Americanise Shotton and tried to steamroller the workers into his ways. Naturally they resented what they regarded as outside interference.

Relations between Summers and their workers had remained remarkably good during this difficult time of transition and experimentation. Production techniques had always been discussed at great length and in great detail. But the firm had to manage the plant and make it pay and the unions had to protect the wages and conditions of work of their members and both sides respected the other's position. During the depression of the 1920s the unions were relatively weak and the firm's finances were tight, but meetings continued and the lines of communication remained open.

Now Hoover and his management team wanted to set up an advisory committee of operatives rather than deal with the union officials. They actually thought that bonuses of sweets and chocolates would be acceptable for good output.

Relations between men and management became strained. Here, at least, was an area in which Geoffrey's talents could be used. He thankfully left the technical decisions to Hoover but listened sympathetically to the workers' complaints and tactfully intervened on their behalf, thus averting any serious breakdown.

While all this was going on, export markets were dwindling as countries such as India, Japan and Australia, who had always bought their steel sheets from Britain, now began to build their own steelworks. Lack of business led, in 1929, to the closing down of the rolling mills at the old Globe Iron Works.

Some workers moved over to the Shotton works. The nail works stayed open and production of cut nails remained a steady trade, but the outlook for John Summers & Sons, for the country, indeed for the world, was bleak. The Wall Street crash hit America on 24 October 1929, and on that day of panic selling thirteen million shares changed hands. The depression spread across the Atlantic and European markets were disrupted. For the next five years it was a downward economic spiral on both sides of the Atlantic.

Bruce Gardner, H.S.'s bright young director who had carried through the expansion at Shotton in the First World War, was now in charge of the Shelton Works, which had been bought in the expansion days of 1920, but in 1930 he resigned in order to take an important post in finance and banking. H.S. could never understand why anyone should want to leave his company. What could be more fascinating than making steel sheets? Five years later, he commented, 'I can only think that we did not move fast enough for him, and we could not provide sufficient scope for his great energies and ambitions.'

The moment was ripe for the arrival into the Summers Camp of the next outsider. He was Neville Rollason, who was to become a godsend to H.S. and a lifelong support to Richard. The two young men had remained close friends after student days at Cambridge when each had gone into his father's business. Neville's family firm was the Rollason Wire Co. Ltd., manufacturers of high tensile wire in the Midlands. It was a smaller concern than John Summers & Sons and, as his brother was already in the firm, Neville was much more

Neville Rollason took charge of the Shelton Works in 1930.

interested in the exciting challenges that he sensed in partnership with Richard, who persuaded his father to fill the vacancy in the Shelton management with Neville.

Neville was now in charge at Shelton, Reith Gray and Spencer Summers at Shotton, under the eye of Hoover, with Geoffrey as general manager. Richard, still responsible for the Castle Fire Brick Company, took on the job of managing the transport of the steel sheets by road, rail and sea.

H.S. decided to step in when he realised that something more than vague indefinite statements were needed to explain away the £18,000 loss in the ARMCO department. He blamed himself as much as anyone for not keeping a tighter hold on events and for expecting too much too soon of Geoffrey, whom he dearly wanted to take his place.

Although Geoffrey was ten years older than the others, his technical know-how was no greater, his commitment was, if anything, less and his ability for decision making had dwindled since working for his father. H.S. gave him fatherly advice; 'I don't want you to feel discouraged or disheartened but I do want you to realise the errors of the past which I do not think you have properly appreciated up to now.'

Geoffrey was being battered at work and at home. Past errors were crowding in on him from all sides. His marriage, begun in 1915 when he was a young man of twenty-four, had brought increasing problems. He had never been close to his children and had not found the joys in family life that Richard was experiencing.

His twin son Anthony had undergone a mastoid operation on the kitchen table when he was ten. This sort of thing was common enough but there were complications, and Anthony suffered afterwards from epileptic fists. Geoffrey and his wife could not cope and their son was sent to a special home for the handicapped. Their present nanny, Margaret, who had been with them for a number of years, found that she could no longer handle the other twin, Roland, and so he was sent to be looked after by a family in Tunbridge Wells until he was old enough to go to Shrewsbury School. Meanwhile, daughter Anne was a weekly boarder at a nearby school; in the holidays she was often farmed out to sympathetic aunts. Geoffrey's home life was miserable and he turned, increasingly, to Margaret to share his troubles. He was a gentle man, effortlessly attractive to women, which sometimes bewildered him.

Geoffrey's marriage ended in divorce in 1930 and the next year, on 14 August, he married Margaret, but not with his father's approval. H.S. felt that Geoffrey was far too much under the influence of his new wife. Nevertheless he made them welcome at Cornist Hall where he had lived with a housekeeper

Geoffrey, H.S.'s eldest son.

since Marjorie had left. Geoffrey seemed to want to make Cornist his permanent home and H.S. did not object. He was now sixty-six and spending much of his time in London and in Harrogate where he had found a comfortable hotel and a friendly companion in Mrs Edna Ellis who cared for him for the rest of his life and gave him the affection and loyalty that he had lacked for so many years. As long as he had a bed to call his own at Cornist he was content.

So Geoffrey and Margaret moved into Cornist Hall, which was not perhaps the ideal base for their new marriage. It held too many reminders of Marjorie and her flamboyant lifestyle with H.S., which certainly was not Geoffrey's style.

Meanwhile no one escaped a few home truths from H.S.:

> The works is not a playground. There is no substitute for hard work. There is not that proper supervision that there ought to be and if you find slackness at the top you are likely to find it all the way down. I don't know why you all three, Geoffrey, Richard and Spencer went to London yesterday; this works ought not to be left to look after itself when Mr Buckley is away.
>
> Once you allow slackness to prevail it is hard to root it out. I should say that there is hardly a department in the works where considerable economies cannot be affected.

H.S. brought out of retirement John Sidebottom in a desperate attempt to stop the downward slide of the Summers fortunes. John had come to the Globe Iron Works at Stalybridge as a boy in the times of Trevelyan Sharp, and through hard work and loyalty had risen to be in complete charge of the Globe Iron Works. When the sheet mills closed down in 1929, John had retired.

H.S. recommended John Sidebottom to Geoffrey as the man whose experience and mature judgement best fitted him to give guidance 'worth everything else that you will find'.

Mr Sidebottom was given the disagreeable job of clearing up hundreds of tons of defective steel sheets which had to be got rid of at any price. But in spite of all efforts, economic forces were against them.

On 24 April 1931, known afterwards as Black Friday, the steelmaking plant was entirely closed down and more than four thousand men out of a workforce of six thousand were sacked. The sheet mills kept rolling with a much reduced output.

In the afternoon the envelopes came round. Inside each was a letter from H.S.:

> . . . The last few weeks have been the most unpleasant and anxious that the Directors have ever had to face. They realise that in the action they are now

taking they have to tell many of the firm's most loyal servants that there is
no more work for them.

They have studied every individual case, and, whilst it is hard to
dispense with those who have rendered faithful service to the company for
many years, they feel that, in the interests of the firm, no other course is
open to them. . . . You will, however, be paid two weeks salary in lieu of
notice.

H.S. blamed his drastic step on Continental firms being allowed to dump their
surplus steel in the country at prices with which it was impossible to compete.
He had been forced to buy this cheaper steel rather than continue to produce
his own. He also laid responsibility on the high taxation under which English
firms were labouring, and the rates of wages and standards of living that
workers had come to expect.

Added to this, foreign firms were sheltered by high tariffs. But in 1932 at the
Ottawa Conference, a new system of tariffs and imperial preference was
augmented that was to last until the 1970s. A century of free trade came to an
end. There to witness it and to represent the steel sheet industry on the steel
trade advisory committee was Geoffrey Summers.

In order to preserve what business they could – exports were 25 percent of
what they had been – the firm had to reorganise the rolling mills on a
diminished output. The works were reduced to one engine, the size it had been
in 1896. Neville was brought over from Shelton to bring his fine business
brain to bear on the ailing works at Shotton and John Sidebottom was once
more called upon, this time to manage Shelton temporarily.

Just at this time, when John Summers & Sons was desperately looking for
ways to relieve the economic gloom, a ray of hope appeared on the horizon in
the shape of an order for galvanised sheets from the Argentine government.
They were to be used as a barrier against the threatened invasion of locusts,
and speedy delivery was essential before the locusts grew their wings.

The idea was to stand the sheets upright. The locusts were unable to climb
over them, and after crawling and struggling, died in their thousands. They
were then shovelled up and their bodies burned. It was an ingenious solution
which solved many of Summers' problems, too.

The order was for 22,700 tons of sheets and was given to the members of the
Sheetmakers' Conference, of which Henry Summers was chairman. As John
Summers & Sons were by far the largest producers of galvanised sheets they
were in a position to marshal their forces quickly and profit most. H.S. made
all the arrangements for shipping, distribution, financing etc.

The order was a welcome spur to the industrial revival just beginning to
emerge on Deeside. On 31 October 1933, the *North Wales Guardian* was able to
report: 'The great steel works and rolling mills of John Summers & Sons at
Hawarden Bridge are now in active operation.'

A view of the works in the 1930s.

Throughout the summer of 1934 Neville was hard at work in the ARMCO department. Richard had been busily involved with extensions of the Buckley brickworks while still managing the transport side of the business. He was also working closely with Neville. One morning H.S. arrived at the works, marched into the office, summoned Hoover and told the American that his services were no longer required. H.S. could take no more losses. Geoffrey retired to the sidelines, bruised but relieved that he had not had to take the tough action.

Neville was put in control and after only a week H.S. was jubilant; 'Already economies have been effected which will save £25,000 a year. In a month I expect this figure will have grown to £50,000. Then he will start on improvements from which it is expected that another £50,000 will be reaped.'

Geoffrey waited for the family, and Neville, to decide what his future role should be. H.S. wrote to Richard in September of this year, 'It would be much more satisfactory for him if his duties could be defined . . . You might talk it over with Neville.'

Henry Hall Summers celebrated his seventieth birthday on 25 January 1935. It was a celebration in spite of recent troubles. There were, after all, signs for optimism – output was rising, dividends were slightly up and the Shelton Works had achieved a record year with a full order book for 1935.

And so a dinner was arranged at the Grosvenor Hotel, Chester, by the company's directors. The original number of five hundred invitations eventually settled at just over two hundred, of which one hundred and twenty were staff from Shotton. Five Summers men were present, Geoffrey, Richard and Spencer of the third generation, Walter in the chair and Harry in the seat of honour.

The opening speech of welcome was made by Mr W. M. Evans, J.P., who could remember John Summers & Sons coming to Shotton nearly forty years earlier. He spoke in high praise of H.S.:

> From time to time are born men who are destined to achieve great things, men who stand apart from their contemporaries, men who are exceptionally endowed with a rare combination of gifts to an unusual degree. These men are not measured by ordinary standards, nor can they be explained – they simply are. They belong to an exclusive category, and to these men we apply the word, 'genius'. We are very glad, Mr Chairman, of this opportunity to pay our homage and respect to one who is, by general consent, unquestionably a member of that select company.

Many of the guests were retired employees who had given their working lives to the Summers firm. H.S. told them that he did not regard their pensions as 'charitable gratuities; they are the reward for faithful services rendered in the

H.S. celebrated his seventieth birthday on 25 January 1935.

past'. He wanted to mark his seventieth birthday by a gift to his workmen and he decided to give them a clubhouse where they could meet for bowls and gossip. He, in return, was given an eighteenth-century silver tankard and a modern silver salver from the works staff, and from his fellow directors a modern silver dish engraved with a Latin inscription which, in translation, read: 'Be brave in trouble; meet distress with dauntless front; but when the gale too prosperous blows, be wise no less, and shorten sail.'

Once the praises had been sung, toasts drunk, gifts presented and compliments exchanged, everyone sat back to be entertained by:

    Robert Harbin, Illusionist.
    J. E. Chantler, Tenor.
    J. Wilford Roberts, Baritone.
    Will Morris, Ventriloquist & Entertainer.
    Edgar Patchett, Accompanist.

It was midnight before the party ended.

In his birthday speech H.S. had declared, 'All my energy is still devoted to the service of the Company of which I am chairman.' He was still very much in control, consulted on every move by Neville and Richard as they fought back from the disasters in the high grade sheet department.

After much family discussion, Geoffrey had been left in charge of the original nailworks at Stalybridge and given the job of director in charge of labour relations. It was a task for which he was well suited as he had the confidence of the unions and the workers. Geoffrey knew many of the union officials, national as well as local, through his work on the two labour boards, the Sheet Trade Board and the Galvanising Board. He was to be chairman on both of these boards for over thirty years.

H.S. was glad that a useful place had been found for his eldest son in the business. He confided in Richard, 'There is a lot of useful work which Geoffrey can do for us. The progress of socialism and the reorganisation under Duncan [Sir Andrew Duncan] want careful watching, and I think Geoffrey can do these things very well.'

Geoffrey's job was one worth tackling. John Summers & Sons and their associated companies now employed 14,500 people, with a wages bill of £44,000 a week.

As long as Geoffrey confined his activities to labour matters, cousin Spencer, who had become a director in 1931, was content – but he doubted whether Geoffrey's ambitions would rest in this limited sphere. He also felt that Geoffrey should take a cut in salary to allow for his less responsible role, and to compensate for the rise in salary being given to Neville for taking on extra responsibilities.

H.S. was not prepared to go along with Spencer's suggestions. He thought that Geoffrey had suffered quite enough and he knew the (in his eyes) extravagant lifestyle that Geoffrey and Margaret had grown accustomed to could not be pruned easily. As it was, he was contributing nearly a thousand pounds to their annual household budget now that they were living at Cornist Hall.

Meanwhile H.S. kept a close eye on the one now favoured to succeed him, Richard, and Neville, his right-hand man. He was constantly questioning, criticising and praising, all in typically forthright manner.

Letters to Richard were punctuated by encouraging comments such as, 'You realise the problems we have to deal with and I don't think they could be in better hands', and 'In Neville you have a fine example', and 'Neville has got the best brains of anyone in the concern and they are part of a charming personality.'

All hopes were pinned on Neville and he accepted the challenge but he did not want the job. He wrote to Richard: 'The more I think about the problems at Shotton the less they appeal to me . . . but someone has got to delve into them and that is going to mean months and perhaps years of detailed and tedious work.'

For many reasons he saw it as 'quite the worst job in the world for me'. His personal life was in turmoil. Since student days his friendship with Richard and his wife had grown and deepened. Their lives had intertwined and he had fallen in love with his best friend's wife. His love was known to the three of them and accepted with sympathy and understanding.

Neville had buried himself in work at the Shelton plant, sorting out difficulties for the Summers family, supported at all times by Richard's friendship. While at Shelton, and coming to terms with his lonely future, he had often written to Richard, acknowledging his gratitude and his undying friendship:

> I want to make it as clear as I possibly can that your kindness to me has been, still is and always will be fully appreciated . . . As far as my feelings to both of you are concerned I will raise heaven and earth to prevent anything damaging what has been and will remain a really exceptional friendship.

Neville's private miseries and personal loneliness would have broken a weaker man but his strength of character, appreciated by H.S., gave him inner resources on which he could draw when the Summers family were depending on him. He could count on being a welcome visitor at Richard's happy home, where the fourth generation of Summers sons were growing up. By March 1936 there were three boys and a fourth arrived two years later.

Neville now returned full-time to Shotton to a situation from which he had made such great efforts to escape. He appealed to Richard to release him as soon as was reasonably possible: 'It is going to take a colossal effort to get it [Shotton] back on the proper course again and you must be prepared to exert yourself to the limit when you consider your privileged position and family interests.'

Neville knew that his task was to hold the Shotton fortunes steady until Richard had the confidence in his own unquestionable ability to take over full charge: 'Your father made the business and you must show that you can manage it before you are eligible for perhaps the chairmanship . . . Nothing would please him more than to see his own son again in charge of the parent works.'

Richard was willing to play his part but he was well aware of his own limitations. He had seen Geoffrey fall down on the job and knew that he and his brother had similarities in their make-up. Neither had been well trained in the technical side of steelmaking, and both had had their confidence and self-assurance weakened by years of working under the overpowering presence of their father.

Richard resisted the pressure that Neville was trying to put on him to take on the job of running Shotton on his own at this stage. He gave Neville a list of his doubts:

1. I am far too sensitive and I very easily get depressed. My chief aim in life is my home and my family, these are paramount, if anything is wrong there I am no good.
2. Coupled with this is my health. I seldom know what it is to feel really well and energetic and any sort of worry, especially about the family, aggravates this condition.
3. By nature I want variety. I am not a plodder. I don't want to shirk responsibility but I don't think I should be fair to those who rely on us for their living or to myself if I said I could do something I am not suited for.

Richard was prepared to take on more responsibility as long as he could depend on Neville's support. There were two overriding priorities on which he agreed with his father:

1. Those most suited must be in the right places. This must come before relationships and personal feelings.
2. The company's affairs and policy must be controlled by a Summers for the good of all concerned.

Spencer and Geoffrey were not wholehearted in their commitment to the Summers works. Geoffrey thought that he might play a part in public affairs and toyed with the idea of a seat in the House of Commons, attracted by the prestige and power. Spencer was ambitious, and regarded his present position as a stepping stone to higher things. He was a politician more than a steelmaker.

H.S. was aware of this undercurrent of dreams and ambitions and he realised that men in high places, with the interests of Summers at heart, would be of invaluable help in the future. Meanwhile, as he told Richard in a letter, dated 24 October 1936, 'I think we have got them into the niches which suit them and I am satisfied that they can perform the duties assigned to them with complete satisfaction.'

Since the Ottawa Conference of 1932, the steel industry had been protected by tariffs which benefited the rapidly expanding motorcar industry as it looked to the British Empire for its export markets. Cars were no longer made out of panelled wood frames by coach builders, but out of pressed steel sheets on a production line.

Lifestyles were changing rapidly and everyone wanted the most up-to-date inventions. Washing machines were no longer being made of cast iron, vacuum cleaners were replacing brooms, typewriters and cash registers were commonplace and farmers were mechanising with enthusiasm from feeding troughs to silos, from incubators to combine harvesters – all needing steel.

John Summers & Sons were well placed to supply these more specialised steel sheets by the way they had met and overcome their problems in the years 1928 to 1935. Their policy since 1904, when H.S. had initiated his profit-making scheme, had been to promote able men within their departments so that, now, many of their departmental managers were homegrown.

In 1931, Richard and Spencer, both only twenty-eight, became directors with seats on the board alongside Geoffrey, aged thirty-nine and with ten years experience in the board-room. Neville joined them in 1933. When Richard became vice-chairman in 1935, there were five Summers men on the board of ten. H.S., nearly seventy-one, and Walter, seventy-two, were of the older generation; Geoffrey, Richard and Spencer were of the new.

Although Reith Gray was not on the board of directors at this time, he was nevertheless a force to be reckoned with at Shotton. While Richard and Neville moved into the policy-making seats of power, Reith Gray remained at the works as the supreme operator. He was manager of the high grade sheet mill and he knew every aspect of steelmaking. He also knew the men under him, their strengths and weaknesses and how to stimulate them to maximum endeavours.

Neville was the clear thinker, able to view problems from different angles. He was a quiet man who kept in the background but had the flair to take the crucial decisions and to get them right. Reith Gray was the technical expert, expecting the same high standards from everyone whether employees or colleagues. He scorned incompetence and amateurism, and this included

Richard's lack of technical knowledge. Richard was the co-ordinator and he was a Summers. The three-man team was aided and abetted by Kenneth Younghusband, the electrical engineer who helped H.S. with his grandfather clocks and was Richard's cousin.

There were limits to what could be done by hot rolling processes, and to produce sufficiently thin, uniformly flat and flexible sheets a cold reduction process was necessary. The first major breakthrough came in 1936 when it was decided to install a Sendzimir Mill, which was a Polish invention.

Kenneth Younghusband went over to Germany to see one in action and to meet Mr Sendzimir, who willingly helped and advised the Shotton team. Once the decision was made to invest in one of his mills, Mr Sendzimir came over to Shotton to give the young team the benefit of his experience. The Sendzimir Mill installed at Shotton was the first of its kind in Britain, capable of cold rolling steel sheets up to forty inches wide.

The next big step forward came with the introduction of a continuous hot dipped galvanising line a year later. This again was the first in Britain, the only other one in the world being in Poland. The new zinc-coated sheet was marketed under the trade name of 'Galvatite'. From this sheet everyday practicalities such as buckets, dustbins, wheelbarrows could be made in a straight process without damage to the evenly coated sheet, and no further treatment was needed.

It was an exciting time for the three-man team who were mapping out new boundaries in steelmaking. There were many difficulties and setbacks, and each man contributed in his own way.

H.S. had no intention of being left behind by the new technology and demanded information at all levels. 'In regard to the rollspeed and the velocity of the bar or sheet entering and leaving the rolls . . . we were wrong and I would like a theoretical explanation of the action,' he wrote to one departmental manager.

He was sceptical of the new Sendzimir Mill and gave his opinion in true style:

> As soon as the orders on hand are completed it should be entirely shut down . . . I presume that all the mechanical troubles and defects have now been eliminated, if not, the time must be near when you should stop trying . . .
>
> We cannot have our key men wasting their time on a machine which does not possess the first essentials for any kind of success.

One of the key men was Reith Gray who had rolled up his sleeves and got down to the job of mastering the new machinery. He was determined to overcome all obstacles. One of his workmen recalled:

I thought at times that he would have to give in, but he never would. Often we had to ring him at two and three in the morning and within half an hour he would be on the plant. Where production and development was concerned he was the driving force.

As early as 1925 the world's first hot strip mill had been installed at Ashland in America and, two years later, Geoffrey had gone over with a fellow-director to inspect it. On his return a meeting had been arranged with union officials at the works and H. S. had told them,

> We don't want you to feel that we are hatching any schemes to spring on you without warning; we are not, and we want to keep you informed . . . Sooner or later the change must come . . . when it does, be it next year or five years hence, we look for your assistance and support and you can depend upon us to protect your interests as well as our own.*

In 1935 another visit was made to America to look again at their strip mills, but the Summers board hesitated to make a decision that would involve the company in their greatest capital outlay of all time. John Summers & Sons was a family business and the family wanted to keep it that way; they were well aware that a continuous strip mill could not be financed internally.

They also knew that a continuous rolling mill would bring abrupt changes in jobs and skills, and could lead to a laying off of men at the time when unemployment in the country was a worrying reality. Within the works, there had been enough disruption in recent years over the changes in working methods introduced by the American, Hoover, and when he had left, everyone had breathed a sigh of relief and management had worked hard to re-create an atmosphere of stability and peace.

In 1936, the first continuous strip mill in this country was installed by the Richard Thomas Company at Ebbw Vale in South Wales. A decision could no longer be delayed by Summers and the next year, in March 1937, Richard and Neville, young men not yet thirty-five, went over to America to investigate for themselves. As they crossed the Atlantic in the *Berengaria* they were well aware of the size of the problem and of the weighty decision to be made at the end of the trip. They were going to inspect every aspect of the strip mill process, discuss and seek advice from the president of the Mesta Machine Company of Pittsburgh, Mr Lorenz Iversen.

They were taken to rolling mills built by Mr Iversen and were immensely impressed by the equipment they were shown and by the helpful advice. Mr Iversen very much wanted to do a deal with Summers; it would be good

---

*P. S. Richards, MA, M Phil., *The Hawarden Bridge, Shotton, Chester Iron & Steel Works of Messrs John Summers & Co.*, 1971–2.

Lorenz Iversen, president of the Mesta Machine Company, Pittsburgh, came to
London in 1937 to advise Summers on building their strip mill.

business for his company and would be his first strip mill outside America.

Richard and Neville were completely won over. They came back determined to find the ways and means of installing a strip mill on Deeside. If they
did not, John Summers & Sons would slip behind in the race for the perfect
steel sheet, and unemployment would grow worse and be more lasting.

But first the money had to be found.

In May 1937 Mr Iversen arrived in London and took rooms at the Savoy
Hotel. He had come to advise Richard and Neville on building their strip mill.
After they had lunched together the first estimate of costs was roughed out in
dollars on hotel notepaper. It added up to ten million.

The next problem was to decide who would take charge of organising the
venture, coordinating plans and designs, planning contracts. None of the
present Summers team had the experience for such responsibility. Mr Iversen
knew a man in Copenhagen who might be interested. A phone call was put
through to him and next day Henrik Oveson flew to London and agreed to
take the job.

Mr Iversen returned to America and Richard went away to discuss with
family and fellow directors how the money could be raised. He was now
firmly in the driving seat and by the next year's AGM he had accepted full

responsibility as chairman of John Summers & Sons. Neville was his managing director, Reith Gray was general manager of the works, with a seat on the board. H.S. was made president.

Finance was not readily available in a country that was emerging from a world slump. In the eyes of the business world Richard was a young, untried quantity. He went round the City 'like a pauper with a begging bowl', as he later put it. This was the true testing time for Richard. The steel world was watching him in case he should falter, but he proved a worthy successor to his father.

The first test pile was driven in September 1937 on a site that had previously been marshland. The whole mill had to be carried on piles, and three-quarters of a million tons of sand were pumped from the River Dee to raise the site level. At times that winter it seemed inconceivable that a strip mill could emerge from the sea of sandy waste.

An army of draughtsmen, machinery builders, building contractors,

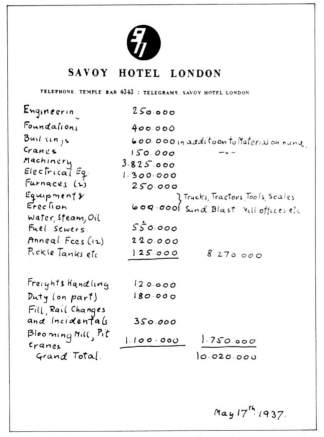

The first estimate of the cost of the strip mill was drawn up on Savoy Hotel notepaper.

engineers and experts from all trades descended on Shotton during the year of 1938.

All this time Richard was shuttling between banking departments, trying to obtain the best deal possible in raising £4 million new capital. The family was not short on advice. His father admonished: 'You cringe too much, you must pose as the top dogs and though we will not ask for anything unreasonable, we will not accept anything that we don't like.'

On the other hand his Uncle Walter admired his skill and advised, 'It is necessary to remember we are not dictators but suppliants.' On 10 January 1939, his father-in-law William Irvine wrote:

> My dear Richard,
>   I must send you a line, now that the news is out, to congratulate you most heartily on your successful negotiation of what I am sure has been a most difficult piece of business.

But H.S. once again was gloomy, saying, 'The terms which it is proposed to thrust on us make me quite ill. Two nights running I have had no sleep.'

H.S. hated the prospect of the family losing control. It must have been a particularly worrying time for him just when he had officially handed over control of his beloved works to his youngest son and vacated the chairman's seat on the board of directors, a seat he had occupied with vigour and with pride for twenty-five years.

The business had always been run by a Summers, ever since his father started making clogs, irons and nails. The next Summers generation had carried the firm into the rolling and making of steel sheets. It was H.S.'s initiative that had taken them from Stalybridge to Shotton, making available the acres of land that would be needed for this new development.

As his sons came into the business H.S. had acquired subsidiary companies upon which steelmaking depended, collieries, brickworks, iron-making plant. These had brought outsiders on to the family board of management but the founder family always remained firmly in control – and in particular Henry Hall Summers.

When the high grade sheet department came into being, it was managed by the American Rolling Mill Company, but the capital structure and control remained Summers'.

The early programme of expansion had turned the family into a limited company in 1898, with a capital of £200,000. Between 1904 and 1920 increases in the capital had taken it to £3,712,000. The chances of raising money for the new strip mill by public issue were slim, and negotiations on the plan for financing it were long and difficult.

Richard did a deal with one of the largest steel combines in the country, the

United Steel Company. This firm had connections in all the main branches of the steel industry, except sheet manufacture, and here was an opportunity for them to plug that gap. They pledged £1.2 million in ordinary shares, impressed by the past record, personality and future promise of Richard and Neville.

Richard's second backer was a financial body controlled by the Bank of England, and they promised a further million in ordinary shares on which United Steel were granted a seven year option.

Richard then raised another £2 million by the issue of debentures. This was made easier by the firm's conservative financial policy over many years.

H.S. did not see why it was necessary to involve the United Steel Company or the Bankers Industrial Development Company, so that they would have a say in the future of his company. But he had to accept that the firm which he had spent his lifetime creating was now too big to carry on in the old way.

Under the new agreement United Steel had a fifth interest in the firm's share capital and two men on the board of directors, a place on their board being given in return to Neville. The £1 million provided by the Bank of England gave them authority as financial supervisors, plus the power to pass any resolution in a general meeting by the creation of one new 'A' share with special voting rights.

Thus control of the company for the next ten years passed to a committee of which the Bank of England's governor would be chairman. The rest of the committee comprised the chairman and deputy governor of the Bank, and the chairmen of John Summers and United Steel. Richard was uncomfortably aware of the power of this extra share, but he relied on Neville's influence on the United Steel's board to back him, should the need ever arise.

It had been a good move in the negotiations to place Neville on United Steel's board. Richard felt that under difficult conditions he had achieved the best possible deal and this view was expressed on all sides. He received many letters of congratulations, and those from men with whom he had been bargaining especially pleased him. They expressed such sentiments as:

I think the United Steel Company are very fortunate in having come into contact with two such outstanding men as yourself and Rollason.

Your fine history will repeat itself in the future.

I really wonder whether even in good times you could have found £4 million on much better terms.

Richard had every right to feel well satisfied with himself.

While Richard was busy raising the necessary capital, Geoffrey, as director in charge of labour relations, was meeting with the unions to discuss the problems that would arise in the new strip mill. In the spring of 1938, he had visited America with a delegation from the Sheet Trade Board and he brought back a film of the continuous rolling mill to show to the men at Shotton. Reith Gray, known and respected by the men whom he had worked alongside, sought to allay their fears over redundancy, and told them that though fewer operatives would be needed on the continuous rolling process, many jobs would be created in other expanding departments.

Huw Edwards, an experienced trade union official and a remarkable man, met the different unions at the works informally and acted as the personal link between them. He later gave this testimony to the family firm: 'Every worker knows in his heart that he will get a square deal and can pursue his case from the shop floor right through to the Managing Director if necessary . . . the name Summers is held in deep and lasting affection.'

On 1 February 1939, an Extraordinary General Meeting was called at which the share capital of the firm was increased from £4 million to £6 million. Richard made his first speech as chairman, and as was to be expected, he expressed his confidence in the new deal and looked with optimism to the future.

Then he and Neville went with Evelyn on a skiing holiday to Switzerland. Even at Klosters his thoughts were not completely free of the momentous decisions that had just been made. He wrote to his father about the deal: 'I do not think this need mean any drastic changes and I hope and believe that the staff will not notice any difference at all.'

H.S. was pleased that he was still being consulted, and replied; 'You must not forget that I have no other interests to serve than the happiness of those who are dear to me and the success of our business upon which they all so much depend.'

But this was no time for sitting smugly back. Gradually twenty-seven acres of marshland had been raised to the necessary level and it was possible to get some idea of where the machinery would go. Reith Gray was in overall charge on the site, coordinating the immense organisation, and was just the man for the job. He was a hard taskmaster, with a tough exterior but a kind spirit underneath. His technical knowledge was profound and respected by the men. His advice was, 'when going from A to B observe everything on the way.'

Some 7,260 tons of machinery had been ordered from America. British engineers did not have the experience of the intricate machinery that would be needed in a modern strip mill, but Richard negotiated hard and a large order went to British firms.

It was arranged that the mill should be brought over in three shiploads, using vessels equipped with gear that would handle large heavy pieces of machinery. The first journey came perilously close to disaster. On 9 March 1939, the MV *Belnor* left Baltimore bound for Birkenhead, carrying 2,517 tons of machinery for delivery to Shotton.

There was a great storm at sea with hurricane squalls. Some cargo was lost overboard and large packages came loose and rolled about on the foredeck. Five days out at sea a distress signal was sent out and the lifeboats were made ready. Oil was pumped overboard to subdue the mountainous waves.

Luckily the weather moderated a little and on 29 March the ship was brought safely to port through the courage and skill of the captain and crew. This was recognised by the Liverpool underwriters who presented the captain with a cheque for £500 for himself and his crew. John Summers & Sons Ltd. gave Captain Cjertsen a gold watch.

Two more shipments were made by 29 May but the replacement of the machinery lost at sea did not arrive until 19 September. By this time we were at war with Germany and there was a risk of the ship being torpedoed.

Almost the entire workforce was inexperienced in strip mill handling and everyone was learning on the job, apart from a handful of Americans sent over from the Mesta Machinery Company. H. J. Kalberkamp had designed much of the machinery and he came over. George F. Paul came too. He had started

Machinery for the new mill was unloaded at Liverpool.

George F. Paul who had set up two strip mills in America, came to England to help
the Summers team.

up two in America, which at the time he had thought enough for any man, but
here he was in England at work on a third. Some of the Summers team had
been over to America to see a strip mill in action, but there was no substitute
for direct experience and they became very fast learners, especially Alfred
Cutts, the chief electrical engineer, and Cyril Bottomley who became directly
responsible for erecting the enormous pieces of machinery.

The great moment came when the first slab could be discharged from the
furnace. It was Thursday, 9 November 1939, and the time was exactly 5.50
p.m. It had been decided to roll after 5 p.m., when most of the workers would
have gone home, so that the inexperienced operators would not be disturbed
by too many spectators and if the first roll were to be a flop, there would not be
many to see. But somehow word had got round and practically all the works
stayed behind to join in the excitement, as one red hot slab after another failed
to complete the course. Some were too thick, some moved too quickly, some
cobbled into grotesque shapes. 'Well, now I guess it looks just like home,' said
George Paul. Within three hours the rolling process had steadied and the new
continuous strip mill was in action.

SIX

The Second War

The Second World War offered a tremendous opportunity for expansion in the steel industry and the top men at Summers led the way. The loss of jobs that Richard had feared, with the installation of the strip mill and with the increased mechanisation that followed, was averted by the outbreak of war. The old hand rolling mills were kept in operation much longer than had been planned and only gradually phased out, until eventually the last mill closed in 1946.

Even before the official declaration of war, the Shotton Works had moved into the production of air-raid shelters. They were made from galvanised corrugated sheets and were known as Anderson shelters. Geoffrey Summers spoke on the wireless about the new shelters that his firm was making and 'why every family should have one'. It was 29 August 1939.

He spoke with enthusiasm of the tests that were going on at Shotton: 'The Home Office let off some 500lb. aerial bombs very close to a group of the shelters at a distance of 25 feet and over. They were hardly disturbed, let alone damaged.' One brave man volunteered to go into the shelter while a heavy concrete ball, normally used for breaking slag, was dropped on it.

The firm had already turned out a million of these shelters and was producing them at the rate of fifty thousand a week, but by 1941 there was a shortage of the zinc used in the galvanising process, and Anderson shelters were superseded by Morrison shelters, which gave indoor protection. There was now considerable over-production of steel sheets, which meant that some sheet mills had to close. Those who remained in production – Summers was one – contributed a levy from which compensation was given to those forced to close.

At the outbreak of war Geoffrey and his cousin Spencer moved further out of the circle of the family works and into public life, but they kept their seats on the board of directors. Spencer became Director for Sheets in Iron and Steel Control, a national appointment which he held until in 1940 he became Unionist MP for Northampton, taking over at a by-election from the resigning MP, Sir M. E. Manningham-Buller. Geoffrey's sphere was local rather than national politics, and he became chairman of Flintshire County Council in 1940, a position held by his Uncle James from 1904 to 1909. H.S. detected many characteristics in common between his eldest son and his eldest brother. He confided to his brother Walter, 'They were both well-meaning and did their best but they were landed in a sphere for which they were not suited.'

Many others moved at the outbreak of war from the family firm, but their

THE "SUMMERS" AIR-RAID SHELTER

NINE POINTS OF INTEREST :

1. The Shelter can be erected by unskilled labour.

2. No bolts, nuts or fastenings requiring tools are required for erection.

3. The right-angle entrance affords complete protection from shell-blast.

4. All doors are of gas-proof construction fitting against felted facings.

5. Allowing 1' 6" per person, the shelter will hold 4 persons per yard of length, that is 35¼ cubic feet of air per person.

6. Cubic capacity per foot of length—47 cubic feet.

7. Weight of one curved sheet : about 73 lbs.

8. Weight of end of " Z " bar frame : about 144 lbs.

9. 3' 6" depth of excavation is sufficient to cover shelter with 2' 0" of earth per foot of length.

Even before the declaration of war on 3 September 1939, John Summers & Sons was producing air-raid shelters.

move was not of their choosing. Some 1,834 men went into the armed forces and many of their places were taken up by women answering the nation's call to duty. There had been women working in the general office since the First World War, but now they moved into the laboratories, the packaging departments, and even on to the cranes. At first the men jealously guarded their roles, but they came to respect the women's courage and common sense.

Eleanor Bishop was appointed as welfare officer to the women and 'spent five years of what was the happiest time' of her life at Summers works. After the war she looked back with affection in the local newspaper:

> The girls would tackle anything and they stuck really monotonous jobs better than men . . . Some of them weren't above pinching the plugs from the washbasins or the lavatory chains, and electric light bulbs were apt to take wings but taking them all round they would do anything to help anyone who was in real trouble, and they never hesitated to air their grievances either with me or with the 'bosses' who were always ready to listen . . . Morals were certainly unpredictable and the crane drivers had some hair raising tales about what went on in some of the waggons . . . I remember a young woman who had produced three illegitimate children by the same man and who came to ask me whether I thought she could get another affiliation order. 'He's not married, is he, Mary?' I asked. 'No,' she said, so I asked her why, as this was the case, she didn't marry him. 'Why,' she replied with a surprised look, 'I don't like him.'

The welfare officer learnt one valuable lesson, never to be surprised at anything at all.

Women never penetrated into the strip mill, the pickling or annealing plants, the foundries or furnaces. As one employee put it, 'You couldn't expect women to work in those conditions. At night the buildings were blacked out with metal sheets so that the inside was as hot as hell and as black as Hades.'

The men were issued with salt tablets because they sweated so much in the roasting temperatures and airless conditions. It was the mill manager's job to see they took their tablets, and it was easy to recognise those who forgot by their grey pallor and unsteady movements. They were told in no uncertain terms to take their salt tablets before they fell head-first into the acid tanks.

There was continuous production at the works, day and night, and it was immensely difficult for the glow from the furnaces, ladles and slag pots to be completely shrouded at night. But it had to be done. A system was worked out that would give the workers warning when they were not to tap out the furnaces, as this action sent a glare into the sky that was visible for miles. At the centre of the works was the telephone headquarters, manned twenty-four hours a day. From here, word went out to the departmental managers whenever enemy aircraft were sighted, heading towards Deeside. No one knew where the brunt of the attack would be felt, but no chances were taken. A purple warning light, flashed round the works, told the men to go to the shelters. A red flashing light meant take immediate cover.

Shotton Steelworks was very lucky not to receive a single direct hit throughout the war. John Summers & Sons was certainly known to the German Luftwaffe, as shown by a map dated September 1941 that was retrieved from a German plane, brought down nearby. The works were protected by the Clwyd mountain range, which made low-flying raids hazardous, and by the strategy of placing decoy lights out on the marshes and on the bracken slopes of the Welsh hills. One important decoy light was placed right by Richard's home on the Wirral side of the Dee estuary. This would light up his home when everyone else's was shrouded in blackness, and Richard decided it would be prudent to evacuate his family for a while to a less conspicuous spot, so Evelyn moved home to the Welsh side of the Dee. There was just an occasional stray plane that either by bad or perfect navigation found its way up the estuary to Shotton, and a Spitfire from Sealand Aerodrome or a Hurricane from Hawarden Aerodrome was hurriedly sent up to dispatch it.

At first, protection for those at home was provided by the Local Defence Volunteers, and then the Home Guard organised by Colonel Marsden, a regular army officer, took over. The works had their own regiment, which included the men from Bees Nurseries, the bulb and seed firm that grew vegetables instead of flowers in the war. Curiously, the regiment, about 1,600 strong, became the 19th Cheshire Regiment, although the men who formed it were Welshmen and Shotton was in Flintshire. Still, Richard was chairman of Shotton Steelworks, and he lived in Cheshire and became colonel of the regiment.

There were four companies under the command of the senior management. The companies were subdivided into platoons of seventy-two men, and these were commanded by men with experience in the First World War.

Richard took his responsibilities as colonel seriously. Geoffrey was a company commander, but he decided it was not the job for him and resigned. Not just anyone could join the Home Guard; those with a police record were turned down straight away. Discipline was strict and drill was taken seriously, even though at first it was done with pickaxes. Twice a week there was rifle training at Chester Barracks, and the men were taken there and back from the works by bus.

Patrol exercises went on round the works and out at Bees Nurseries – which provided a good chance for the Home Guard gardener to stuff his pockets with tulip bulbs that had been dug up and piled negligently on the land that was now turned over to vegetables.

Richard (front right) joined the works' Home Guard and became the colonel of the regiment.

Women came into the first-aid rooms during the war, and here again they initially met resistance. The workers did not like being treated by women and had to be pushed and persuaded to go for treatment. It was a different scene from ten years earlier, when Charlie Albert Evans had been in charge of the ambulance room. He had done his best with iodine for cuts, picric acid for burns and lead and opium lotion for sprains. More serious cases went to Chester Royal Infirmary. In his free time Mr Evans was a magician, and everyone at the works knew him as Charlie Albert the Conjurer. A poster on the wall of his first aid room read: 'Don't come here for Evans sake, Come for your own.'

As the men went off to war and women took over a number of jobs that had by tradition belonged to the men, it was difficult to stop even skilled steelmakers from feeling that they were not doing enough for their country. Many became restless. Richard felt that the people needed to know that their efforts were vital to the war effort and he had the idea of putting up a shop window, exhibiting all the products that John Summers workers were contributing to the war. This was subject to clearance by security, but Richard felt that his workers were entitled to feel proud of their achievements. It was also an effective propaganda excercise to keep the workforce hard at it.

Geoffrey contributed in his capacity as chairman of Flintshire County Council by taking all his fellow officials on a guided tour of the works. Richard and Reith Gray were on hand to act as guides and the wives were brought in to help too.

Neville at this time was far too busy to participate in the public relations work. He had been loaned to the United Steel Company in a part-time role as managing director to help them out of a difficult situation on the sudden death of their own MD. Neville was also still MD at John Summers & Sons and Richard as chairman did not want this arrangement to change. However they both felt that the present loan arrangement would help United Steel and also strengthen the ties between the two companies, and would therefore be in the national interest.

The only person not pleased by the arrangement was the governor of the Bank of England who, since February 1939, held the power of the controlling share in John Summers & Sons. Richard, uncomfortably aware of this power, was called to a meeting with the governor, who made plain his views that Neville could not serve 'both God and Mammon'.

Richard was determined not to lose Neville and equally determined not to be pushed into the managing director's chair himself, as that would leave his seat vacant for a nominee appointed by the governor. The Summers board backed Richard, and after two months of meetings and mediation, the governor agreed that Neville Rollason would return to Summers once United Steel had been able to make 'suitable permanent rearrangements'.

Richard was furious that what he regarded as narrow, blinkered thoughts could occupy the minds of so many in these times of emergency and he looked back in later years with these comments, 'The chief lesson to be learned is that one should not get oneself into a position where any one person, or small body of persons, can dictate the major policy of the company.'

So Neville stayed with United Steel until June 1941 and then went back to the Summers camp. Morale at the Shelton Works was given a tremendous boost in February of that year by a visit from King George VI and Queen Elizabeth, and Neville was there to conduct them round the works. The very next year, the royal couple came to Deeside and toured the Shotton Works. The King inspected the Home Guard platoon and Geoffrey was honoured with the CBE. There to watch the happy occasion were Geoffrey's wife Margaret and their two young daughters.

It was not only Summers men and women and Summers steel that helped in the war effort; Summers ships also played a vital part. Many of their fleet of approximately twenty were commandeered by the government and used as petrol carriers. Two were requisitioned by the Royal Navy and one was used as a buoy boat by the Royal Air Force. The SS *Maurita*, a single screw steamer, had been sold to a Lancaster firm in 1935 but, strangely, she met her end in

King George VI, accompanied by Neville Rollason, and Queen Elizabeth, with
Richard Summers, visited the works in February 1941.

wartime not far from the Shotton Works when she was mined in the Dee
estuary, and all the crew were lost.

The two newest motor vessels of the Summers fleet, built in 1940, were
fitted out with guns at Liverpool, ready to play their part in the Normandy
landings. The *Staley Bridge* was attached to the American forces detailed to
land at Arromanches, and the *Hawarden Bridge* was the first Allied ship to enter
Dunkirk harbour after the town's liberation.

John Summers & Sons had every right to feel proud of their contribution
towards the defence of their country. In Richard's statement as chairman on 22
May 1945, he announced: 'We have been working at very high pressure for the
last six years, producing some 3,350,000 tons of ingots . . . and 2,220,000 tons
of sheets . . . sufficient to make over 60,000,000 steel and ammunition boxes,
over 40,000,000 jerricans and 16,000,000 drums of petrol and oil.'

As the war drew to a close, so did the life of Henry Hall Summers. His last
surviving brother, Walter, died in May 1944. Harry now made sure that his
affairs were in order. After Walter's death he left instructions for his two sons:
'I think I would like to lie at Mottram beside your angelic mother and our
beloved Gordon.'

His lifelong concerns had been his firm and his family, his family and his firm. They were inextricably bound together and in Harry's mind and heart one equalled the other. His death in January 1945 was recorded in the *Ashton Reporter* with this testimony, 'A more fearless, a more honest and more straightforward man it would be hard to name.' These were qualities that Harry had always respected. In March 1939 he had written: 'I am more proud than of anything else of the fact that I can with truth say that whatever I have achieved, I have never departed, or suggested or induced anyone else to depart from the highest standards of commercial integrity.'

SEVEN

The End

The war years had meant a delay in the ambitious plans to turn Shotton into a fully integrated plant, but now that war was over, the young men and women came out of the forces and back to the works to join those who had been running the continuous strip mill. These men had served a hard apprenticeship under Reith Gray, and if they had not come up to H.S.'s standards, they were not promoted to head their departments. H.S. had always worked a minimum six-day week and he expected the same from his managers. No excuse was accepted for absence at the Saturday morning meetings, and no one left until all the problems had been discussed and decisions taken.

H.S.'s fascination with steelmaking lived on in the post-war generation, who brought a new technical efficiency and expertise into the firm and formed a new tier of management. Richard had inherited his father's chair but it was an entirely different arrangement. He was completely dependent on his managing director, Neville Rollason, his general manager, Reith Gray, and his company secretary, James MacMillan, who had taken over in 1941 when Mr W. M. Bancroft retired after thirty-three years as company secretary. They, in their turn, were dependent on the departmental managers, each of whom was an expert in his field. Together, as the family company of John Summers & Sons, they were part of a national plan for steel, co-ordinated through the Iron & Steel Board and the British Iron & Steel Federation.

During the war, Geoffrey, H.S.'s eldest son, and Spencer, Frank's youngest, had moved to the periphery of the team at Shotton and as H.S. had predicted, their future ambitions did not lie in steel. Geoffrey was committed to local politics, and after the war he became chairman for the Conservative Party of the Wales and Monmouth area. In 1948, he reached the height of his political career when he presided over the sixty-ninth annual Conservative Conference at Llandudno.

Spencer did not return to steelmaking either, although, like Geoffrey, he kept his seat on the board of directors, except for one year towards the end of the war when, for political reasons, he had to relinquish it. In 1950 he was elected Conservative MP for Aylesbury and stayed there very comfortably for the next twenty years. He was particularly proud of his achievement as one of the founders of the Atlantic College, Glamorgan, an international educational establishment.

In 1945, a Labour government was elected and pledged to nationalisation. As chairman of John Summers & Sons, Richard was drawn into political battles, which he found irksome as they prevented him from getting on with what he regarded as his main job, namely keeping ahead of world competition in steelmaking. He opposed the nationalisation of the collieries and spoke against it in May 1946:

> We don't know when our pits will be taken from us, nor do we know what we are likely to receive in compensation for this loss . . . No compensation in money can make good to us the loss that we shall suffer by giving up that intimate control over the pits which has been such an advantage to us as iron and steel makers.

The National Coal Board took over on 1 January 1947 and two years later it was the turn of steel. In his statement to the Annual General Meeting of shareholders on 25 May 1949, Richard made it clear that in his opinion the implementation of the Iron and Steel Bill, which gave to the state the power to take over the whole of the company's assets, would be harmful to the industry and to the nation. He could see no benefit in giving control to Whitehall and superimposing an impersonal authority. The slogan at Shotton was, 'STEEL IS SERVING YOU WELL' and so it was, for each year new records were set in steel production.

In 1947 the workforce stood at 5,850 and soon there would be jobs for thousands more. Plans were under way for the construction of more coke ovens and blast furnaces, a new open hearth melting shop with laboratories and maintenance departments, a sinter plant and a chemical plant.

The expansion programme covered the next ten years and the finance budget was set at £54 million. This time there was no need to take a begging bowl around the City. At the end of the war, the United Steel Company had bought out the Bankers Industrial Development Company, so the governor of the Bank of England no longer held the controversial controlling share. Richard and Neville were both on the board of United Steel and there was close cooperation between the two companies. In February 1947, there was an issue of shares in John Summers & Sons to increase the capital holding by £2 million, which would help to cover the immediate development.

The only extravagance allowed was in the use of land, and this was a tribute to H.S.'s foresight when he persuaded his brothers to move to Shotton. Land reclamation had been part of the scheme from the start, but in the early days there had been no big drainage problems. Now it was planned to create two hundred and eighty acres from the Dee marshes, with a firm enough found-ation to support the largest blast furnaces in Europe. The River Dee was to be pushed back to make way for further expansion.

Dutch engineers, expert in land reclamation, were brought in, the only foreigners in a workforce that grew to nine thousand as the acres under construction increased to five hundred and twenty. Six million tons of sand, left behind by the tides of centuries, were pumped on to the site, creating a plateau for the ever-growing works. An entire sandbank opposite Connah's Quay, which H. S. had no doubt skirted in 1895 as he was rowed up the river in order to view the potential for steelmaking, was sucked up by a dredger and deposited on a dry base. Dee sand is very fine, which means that it pumps easily but has to be protected against wind erosion, so the entire area was covered with ashes, which gave good drainage and ensured a dry base for the construction teams, whatever the weather.

Before the work was completed, on 15 February 1951, the government took over the steel industry. On this day, the shares of John Summers & Sons were transferred to the Iron and Steel Corporation. The family firm now belonged to the state although, to the outward eye, daily life continued much as usual and people still spoke of working at Summers. The transfer of assets was the only major change that took place and the country's steel firms were not broken up. Nationalisation was more of a change of ownership than a change of direction.

Six months later political fortunes were reversed in the country and in October a Conservative government, led by Winston Churchill, was returned to power. One of its promises was to repeal the nationalisation of steel, but the government had an elderly, ailing leader and only a small majority, and such pledges would take time to implement.

At Shotton, Reith Gray was the solid, dependable centre of the organisation. He sparked off new, imaginative possibilities for future steelmaking and the men turned to him to unravel technical snags. He kept his eye on the day to day details and, at the same time, on the overall pattern of production. In short, he was overworked but he did not take kindly to suggestions that he should appoint an assistant. The answer was to bring in his son Stephen from steelmaking at Corby. Stephen was twenty-three and had a first class metallurgy degree from Cambridge.

On 29 April 1953 the Duke of Edinburgh officially opened the new steelworks and power station. A special train, bringing invited guests from London, left Euston Station at 8.10 a.m. and 1,230 guests sat down to a celebration lunch at the works.

Richard, as chairman, welcomed the guests who were witnessing 'the completion of the largest scheme of development and expansion in the history of our company'. There were fifteen members of the Summers family scattered among the guests and on the top table, with forty-five VIPs, were Richard and Evelyn and Geoffrey and Margaret, now Sir Geoffrey, Bart., CBE, DL, JP, and Lady Summers. (Richard had to wait another nine years for his knighthood.)

The Duke of Edinburgh spoke of the family's involvement with steel from the time John Summers visited the Crystal Palace Exhibition over a hundred years earlier and bought a machine to manufacture nails. His Royal Highness

On 29 April 1953, the Duke of Edinburgh opened the new steel works and power station at Shotton.

ended with these words, 'Technically, I suppose, it is still Spring, and it may even be raining, but I think it is a perfect Summers day.'

Then everyone trooped out to tour the works. An hour and a half later, it was back for afternoon tea, and at 6 p.m. the train took the London visitors home again.

For Richard and Evelyn, the entertaining continued. On 1 May, all the office staff, husbands and wives were taken on a tour of the new plant and then given supper, and on the next day, 2 May, about five thousand men and women were entertained to tea in the big dining room in the brickstore. Richard wrote in his diary that night: 'It was another lovely day and they all looked well turned out.'

On 1 October 1954, three years after the election, the Conservative government honoured its election promise and Shotton steelworks belonged once again to John Summers & Sons – not that the workers had really noticed any difference, for the bosses had remained the same and now there was another generation of Summers in the family business.

Richard's eldest son, Peter, who had read German and Russian at Cambridge, came into the works in September of this year, having spent a year at Corby learning about iron- and steelmaking. Unlike Stephen Gray, who was the same age, Peter was not a natural steelmaker and it had taken pressure from his family and from his godfather, Neville Rollason, to persuade him that there would be room for his youthful ideals and ambitions within the family firm. However, he accepted the challenge and his first job, devised by Reith Gray as a quick way of learning about the people and purpose of every department, was to draw up a works rubbish disposal project. There was to be no preferential treatment for this eldest son; in fact, Peter trod a thorny path. Whether he did a job well or badly it was shrugged off equally as only to be expected from 'the boss's son'.

The way ahead was now clear for John Summers & Sons Ltd. who were poised to break away in the development of coated steels, marketing new products before their competitors had caught up with the last. For the next ten years they were riding high. The blast furnace, erected in the 1953 expansion, was producing seven thousand tons a week and was the largest in the world outside the USA.

A continuous working week was introduced, which meant that the production lines were never idle and the furnaces never cooled. Targets were set, achieved and reset even higher. Steel sheet was Shotton's main product. When the Sendzimir Mill was installed before the Second World War, there had been experiments with galvanised strip that had led to the marketing of 'Galvatite'. This was soon followed by 'Zintec', a high grade steel sheet, coated with zinc, that did not peel, flake or crack.

New ideas and new products were pioneered throughout the 1950s under the enthusiastic direction of Reith Gray. Experiments continued with differing thicknesses of zinc and plastic, and improved forms were coming out so fast that before a patent could guard against piracy, the Summers team were on to a new product, and their rivals were left reeling at the speed of their innovation.

In 1957, 'Stelvetite', a cold reduced sheet, was introduced. It was coated on one side with plastic and on the other with zinc; it could be manufactured in many different colours and embossings, making it an extremely attractive and versatile product. Its scientific formula was kept a closely guarded secret but its potential was widely advertised and within a month, nearly six thousand enquiries came into Shotton.

In this year the original post-war target of one million ingot tons was exceeded for the first time and a new target of two million was now set. Four more furnaces were built, bringing the number to twelve, all of the basic, fixed, open hearth type that was common at the time in Britain and America.

Profits were good and morale was high among the workers. Many spent a lifetime with the company and by November 1958 two hundred and sixty-one gold watches had been presented to employees with more than fifty years' service.

By now Richard's second son, Tim, was in the works, having followed in Peter's footsteps with a year in steelmaking at Corby, and then into general management. Both sons were under the eye of the general manager, Reith Gray, and they became his assistants. Stephen Gray was appointed to assistant general manager, a nice distinction, for Stephen would eventually be able to move into his father's place.

Tim chose the commercial side of steelmaking and soon became sales director. Peter, however, as Richard's eldest, was not allowed to become identified too closely with any one department as this could have led to an accusation of favouritism. He had to maintain an objectivity and a distance that would enable him to take an overall view of the family business.

The third son, Bill, after the obligatory year's training, this time in Hamilton, Ontario, joined the Shelton Works, which had been under the management of Melvyn Rollason, Neville's brother, since 1944, and was being expanded and modernised at a cost of £18 million pounds. It was not long before Reith Gray brought him over to join the rest of the fourth generation in the works at Shotton.

In 1963 Neville Rollason died after a long illness and Richard lost his greatest friend.

The next year was an election year and a Labour government was narrowly returned. Steel nationalisation was back on the agenda and Richard renewed his battle against it. He felt very strongly that steel was different from other national monopolies; Summers markets were world-wide and the products carrying the name of their company were known and respected by customers whose goodwill was of immeasurable value. He argued that nationalisation would reduce efficiency, damage the harmonious and close relationships that existed with all grades of industry and just bring complications and delays. 'Why not leave well alone,' he cried in 1964, 'and avoid turning it into a state monopoly with all the upheaval and bureaucratic control that would inevitably ensue.'

The 1960s were years of great change in the steel industry. Open hearth furnaces were gradually being replaced by the new processes, basic oxygen and electric arc. Steel demands were becoming increasingly sophisticated and specialised. Shotton's new furnaces, completed only in 1957, had been set a target of two million tons of steel that was never reached. The nearest they came to it was in 1965 when output reached 1,542,607 ingot tons.

The new £60 million plant was not running at full capacity, but even so, John Summers & Sons weathered the recession better than most companies. This was largely due to the efficient, tightly organised methods that had been worked out between management and workers in the 1950s and 1960s; and to the unique location chosen by H.S. in the 1890s, which allowed all the iron and steel processes to be followed on the same site and close to navigable water.

In 1966, there was another general election and a Labour government was returned to office with a large majority.

In 1967 steel was renationalised. This was a radically different operation from the nationalisation of 1951. Under the chairmanship of Lord Melchett, the new British Steel Corporation aimed at being both commercially competitive and socially compassionate, and an example to private industry as enlightened employers.

For John Summers & Sons, whose works now covered nine hundred and eighty acres and employed thirteen thousand men, it was the beginning of the end. Richard's achievements had been accomplished in half the years covered by his father's, but both had given their lives to the iron and steel industry and both had stayed close to their works, physically and emotionally. Now, however, Bill moved out of steelmaking and Tim moved to the London headquarters of the British Steel Corporation, along with Reith Gray's son, Stephen. Richard's fourth son, Mark, had never entered the works so only Peter, his eldest, remained on home ground as personnel director for the Scottish and North-West Group of British Steel.

One employee spoke for all:

> There won't be any John Summers & Sons any more nor reference to 'over yonder' or to 'under the bridge and over the bridge'. There will just be the Shotton Steelworks and that will be that. Mr Geoffrey and Mr Richard, as they are called, knew everyone in the works and called most of them by their Christian names. Will it be the same when it is just the Shotton Steelworks? I doubt it and I regret it and so, I daresay, will a great many people.

John Summers & Sons did their best to foster among their employees a feeling of belonging to the new corporation by introducing a monthly magazine, *Summers News*, free to all who worked at Shotton, Shelton and Stalybridge, but this was merged into *Steel News* after a year.

Sir Richard, knighted in 1963 for services to the steel industry which had culminated in the office of President of the British Iron & Steel Federation in 1960, now became director in charge of the Scottish and North West Group. He never moved from his home on the Wirral, looking towards the chimneys of Shotton and over the Dee marshes and lagoons where the tern, the newly acquired symbol of the British Steel Corporation at Shotton, nests and breeds.

In 1968, after forty years spent in making steel, Richard and Reith Gray retired. Tributes to both poured in from all levels. Of Richard it was said:

> His combination of heredity, experience and knowledge equipped him to be a successful leader of his company. He did not measure success in any

narrow way. It had to include satisfying the customers with quality and service, being a good employer to those working with the firm, a good neighbour to those near the works and giving a reasonable return to those who invested their savings in it.

And of Reith Gray:

> He was one of that scarce class of individuals who knew the importance when seeking efficiency of meticulously watching every detail without ever losing that sense of proportion necessary to keep production flowing. To this mastery of existing processes he coupled an imaginative approach to future possibilities and has always been prepared to encourage development of the very latest ideas.★

Perhaps this is where the Summers story should end, with a thriving industry handed over to the nation, to provide employment and security for the Deeside community. But, as the 1970s unfolded, the movement at Shotton and throughout the steel industry was ever downwards. The slide into unemployment and redundancy gathered momentum and the people of Shotton were powerless to halt it.

In 1972, the Steel Corporation announced a ten-year plan, concentrating steelmaking in Britain in five centres which would be equipped with the latest technology. Shotton, now part of the Strip Mill division, was not one of these centres. Their open hearth furnaces were to phase out with the loss of seven thousand jobs.

There was a vigorous campaign to halt the closures, backed by all thirteen steel unions, but however hard the workers and the unions fought against it, the trend, although delayed several times by the government, could not be reversed. Centralisation was the policy, with all world orders to be placed at a single source. This led to the resignation of Tim Summers and of Stephen Gray, leaving only Peter Summers still working in the steel industry. He was to move a few years later to a separate industry, devoting his energies first to counselling the unemployed and the redundant, and then to encouraging other industries back to Shotton's empty acres.

In these years, as Shotton Steelworks crumbled away, Sir Richard would put in an appearance from time to time, now a powerless figure, a shadow of his former self. He died in 1977 and is buried in his village churchyard across the sands of Dee from his steelworks.

The old Globe Iron Works had closed at Stalybridge in July 1969, ninety-seven years after the iron plaque announcing its establishment was nailed over the entrance. The buildings were sold to a plastics firm. In February 1980,

★ Mr T. R. Craig, MD, BSC, Scottish & NW Group, *Steel News*, September 1968.

An aerial photograph of the works in the 1970s.

iron- and steelmaking ceased at Shotton with the loss of eight thousand jobs. Escalating oil prices and a declining market for strip mill products finally forced the hand of the British Steel Corporation.

The end was particularly sad. John Summers & Sons had prided themselves on the family atmosphere in the works. 'This place,' said a trade union official, 'has a soul. When the firm has made an agreement, whatever the cost, that agreement is kept, both in letter and spirit.' The works had been founded on sons and daughters following, as of right, into jobs held through the generations. The last strike had been in 1910.

When the end came Summers was on strike and the last cast of steel was made without the due recognition or ceremony that the occasion deserved. The last blast furnace was kept warm from Christmas in the hope that work would begin again, but by February the decision was taken not to resume iron and steel production.

Steelmaking is no more at Shotton but the rolling and finishing of steel goes on. The cold rolling mill is the finest in the country and the coatings department is unmatched in Europe. Investment in the site has risen to £110 million with the commission in 1986 of a £30 million hot dip coil coating line. But the steel is made elsewhere – as it was when John Summers passed his works on to his sons over a hundred years ago.

Bibliography

Private family memoirs, diaries and letters in the possession of Peter J. Summers
Privately printed books
    Smith, Gordon, *Full Circle. The story of steelmaking on Deeside*, Dec. 1980
    Summers, Richard F., *The New Mill 1940*

Coustillas, Pierre, *George Gissing at Alderley Edge*, London, 1969
Dobson, Bob, *Concerning Clogs*, Dalesman Book, 1979
Dolby, George, *Charles Dickens as I Knew Him*, London, 1885
Engels, Frederick, *The Condition of the Working Class in England*, Panther Books, 1979, 1st pub. Gt. Brit. 1892
Gissing, Algernon & Ellen (eds), *Letters of George Gissing to Members of His Family*, 1927
Gissing, George, *The Private Papers of Henry Ryecroft*, Harvester Press, 1982, reproduction of first text, London, 1903
Hill, Geoffrey, *Mercian Hymns XXV*, André Deutsch, 1975
Scott, W. H., Banks, J. A., Halsey, A. H., Lupton, T., *Technical Change and Industrial Relations, A study of relations between technical change and the social structure of a large steelworks*, Liverpool University Press, 1956
Sellman, R. R., *Modern British History 1815–1970 A Practical Guide*, London, 1976

Periodicals

Steel News, Sept. 1968
The Journal of the Flintshire Historical Society, Vol. 25, 1971–72, article by P. S. Richards MA, MPhil., 'The Hawarden Bridge, Shotton, Chester Iron & Steel Works of Messrs. John Summers & Co.'

Index

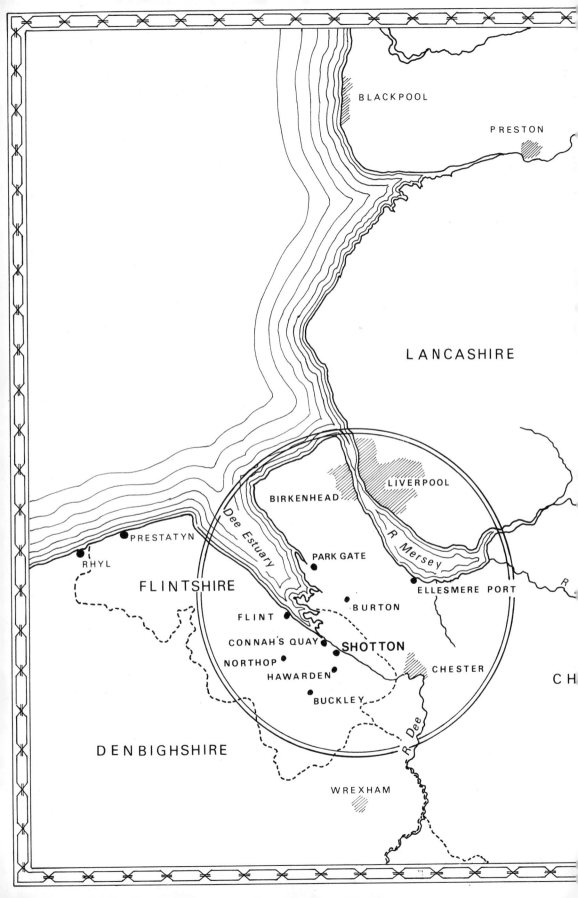

BLACKPOOL

PRESTON

LANCASHIRE

LIVERPOOL

BIRKENHEAD

Dee Estuary

R Mersey

PRESTATYN

PARK GATE

RHYL

ELLESMERE PORT

FLINTSHIRE

BURTON

FLINT

CONNAH'S QUAY

SHOTTON

NORTHOP

HAWARDEN

CHESTER

CH

BUCKLEY

R. Dee

DENBIGHSHIRE

WREXHAM